Vietnam War
River Patrol

Vietnam War River Patrol

A U.S. Gunboat Captain Returns to the Mekong Delta

Richard H. Kirshen

McFarland & Company, Inc., Publishers
Jefferson, North Carolina

LIBRARY OF CONGRESS CATALOGUING-IN-PUBLICATION DATA

Names: Kirshen, Richard H., 1947– author.
Title: Vietnam War river patrol : a U.S. gunboat captain returns to the Mekong Delta / Richard H. Kirshen.
Other titles: U.S. gunboat captain returns to the Mekong Delta
Description: Jefferson, North Carolina : McFarland & Company, Inc., Publishers, 2017 | Includes index.
Identifiers: LCCN 2017000883 | ISBN 9781476668147 (softcover : acid free paper) ∞
Subjects: LCSH: Kirshen, Richard H., 1947– | Vietnam War, 1961–1975—Riverine operations, American. | United States. Mobile Riverine Force—Biography. | United States. Navy—Officers—Biography. | Vietnam War, 1961–1975—Personal narratives, American. | Kirshen, Richard H., 1947– —Travel. | Mekong River Delta (Vietnam and Cambodia)—Description and travel.
Classification: LCC DS558.7 .K57 2017 | DDC 959.704/345 [B] —dc23
LC record available at https://lccn.loc.gov/2017000883

BRITISH LIBRARY CATALOGUING DATA ARE AVAILABLE

ISBN 978-1-4766-6814-7 (print)
ISBN 978-1-4766-2742-7 (ebook)

© 2017 Richard H. Kirshen. All rights reserved

No part of this book may be reproduced or transmitted in any form or by any means, electronic or mechanical, including photocopying or recording, or by any information storage and retrieval system, without permission in writing from the publisher.

Front cover image: a PBR on the Vam Co Tay River; *inset*: the *Avalon Angkor* (photographs from the author's collection)

Printed in the United States of America

*McFarland & Company, Inc., Publishers
Box 611, Jefferson, North Carolina 28640
www.mcfarlandpub.com*

If you are able, save them a place inside you,
And save one backward glance when you are leaving,
for the places they can no longer go.

Be not ashamed to say you loved them,
though you may, or may not have always.
Take what they have left, and what they have
taught you with their dying, and keep it as your own.

And in that time that when men decide, and feel safe,
to call the war insane, take one moment,
to embrace these gentle heroes you left behind.

—Maj. Michael D. O'Donnell,
1 Jan. 1970, Dak To, Vietnam

Table of Contents

Introduction	1
1. First Encounter	3
2. Go Back?	9
3. Flying Follies	12
4. Hong Kong to Saigon	17
5. How the Navy Got Me to Vietnam	19
6. Japan and Overt Sexuality	24
7. Subic Bay, Diving and Coronado	28
8. Prep-Work for War	38
9. Arrival	44
10. How the Hell Had I Ended Up in This Mess Anyway?	45
11. Touring Saigon	49
12. My Initial Introduction to Saigon	60
13. Eating	66
14. Cu Chi, Mr. Nam and the Tunnels	69
15. Operation Giant Slingshot	79
16. The Post Office and the *Angkor*	85
17. Nha Be	88
18. River Jobs	97
19. The Mekong	104
20. The Eskimo	108

21. Visits Along the River	111
22. Fish Farms and Wiping Out a Village	120
23. Cambodia and Night Travel	125
24. Phnom Penh and the Killing Fields	132
25. Our Prisoner	139
26. The Boat Show	142
27. New Life	146
28. Visiting a Cambodian Village	150
29. Again with the Darkness and My Night on the River	157
30. The Fighting Monks	163
31. Zippo Boats and Body Counts	170
32. The Afternoon Trip Without Me	172
33. R & R	175
34. Bus Rides and Ox Carts	179
35. On Watch	184
36. Busses, Goat Roads and Angkor Thom	190
37. Life on the River and Getting Shot	196
38. The Hotel and New Year's Eve	201
39. Cam Ranh Bay	203
40. Angkor Wat and the Citadel of Women	211
41. Bare Sole	215
42. Hanging Out in Town	218
43. The Incidents	223
44. Bangkok and the End of the Trips	228
45. Entertainment	236
46. War?	244
Acronyms and Foreign Words	249
Index	251

Introduction

"Go back to Vietnam? Are you crazy?" It took three agonizing months for me to decide to return to Vietnam, at the urging of my wife and sister, forty-two years after my initial "visit." Returning would entail traversing some of the very same rivers I had patrolled as a boat captain in the U.S. Navy's Mobile Riverine Force during the height of the Vietnam War. Back then, those rivers filled me with fear and apprehension every time I had to journey "up-river." It was with good reason, as the attrition rate attributed to riverine warfare was as high, statistically speaking, as any mission in the war. It was an uncomfortable, dangerous job full of ambushes and unseen dangers that seemed to parallel, in many ways, Joseph Conrad's own trip up-river, in "Heart of Darkness," and of course the cinematic version, Francis Ford Coppola's *Apocalypse Now*.

This book compares the two excursions in a multitude of ways. They range from attitudes to dining experiences; from living conditions to modes of travel; from remembrances of times past to new experiences in the same geographical locations. The trips obviously contrasted with each other, but some things in life never seem to change, and contrast is not always the norm, even through an enormous expanse of time. Photographs from each trip, and each era, are interspersed throughout the narrative to give the reader a perspective about what is written and how some things have changed, while others have remained the same in these two disparate eras.

I grew up in Miami, Florida, the oldest boy in a family consisting of my three younger sisters, a mother who was considerably more liberated than her contemporaries, and a workaholic father who was consistently absent. I completed an AA degree and was drafted into the U.S. Army in 1967, but saw fit to enlist in the Navy the same day I received my draft notice. I thought this would keep me from ending up in Vietnam, or at least on the ground in Vietnam. I couldn't have been more wrong.

1

First Encounter

It was a beautiful day, cloudless, the river still and flat, nary a ripple on the brown mirrored surface. From the jungle, bird noises and the high-pitched resonance of bamboo rubbing against itself filled the air above the exhaust of our low-throttled diesels. I was at the helm as we slowly snaked our way up-river. My engineman, John, from Chicago, was in front of the wheelhouse. He was standing on the other side of the four-foot-high, half-inch-thick, solid steel bulkhead that surrounded me. He was smoking a big bowl of marijuana in a corncob pipe, the scent sweet and pungent as it wafted over me. For some reason, the Navy never put together the anomaly in the Post Exchanges (PXs) that hundreds and

Toking on the LCM-6.

hundreds of Navy men appeared to smoke pipes, but none ever bought any tobacco. Or maybe the upper echelon did get it, and decided that it would be best to just leave it alone. Yeah, that was probably it.

This idyllic tranquil river scene was abruptly interrupted as I spotted a puff of white smoke on the port side of the river floating out of the jungle. Almost instantaneously something flew swiftly across our bow, and exploded violently on the other side of the river. I was perplexed, momentarily at a loss, having only a vague idea as to what had just happened. Then it happened again; the puff of white smoke, the speeding projectile just missing our port bow, and another explosion on the opposite river bank. I leaned over the bulkhead, wild-eyed and screaming at John, "What the hell was that?" He looked up, and back at me over his left shoulder, slowly and deliberately expending his previous toke from the pipe, and with a silly giggling grin on his face said, "It's the fucking war, man."

He was right. That was the first time in my life that anyone had ever tried to kill me. We went to general quarters, grabbed weapons and began to fire back into the jungle. Dennis was on the port side .50-caliber machine gun, Dale on the M-60, John had his M-16, and I quickly picked up the radio and called for air support. I reported my position on the river, requested assistance, and then loaded and re-loaded my M-79 grenade launcher as fast as I could, firing 40MM grenades into the area that I thought the rockets had been launched from. The attack was deafening and terrifying. Every fiber of my very being was alive with the pins and needles of adrenaline coursing through my body like water through a fire hose. We fired back nonstop into the passing jungle.

A scant few minutes later, as we pulled out of firing range after expending hundreds of rounds of ammo, a squadron of helicopters flew low over us. First I heard the thumping of the large blades as they cut the air, a sound that, even to this day, draws my attention and slightly increases my heart rate. Then I saw them. I stared and watched in awe. It was a daunting sight, and I assume unimaginably terrifying to the enemy below.

They were UH-1B (Huey) gunships, and as I watched spellbound, they sent countless rockets, along with M-60 machine gun fire and minigun fire, into the spot we had recently vacated. Each Huey carried AGM-22B wire-guided anti-tank missiles and XM-157 rocket launchers (seven on each side) for 2.75" rockets. A mini-gun is a six-barreled electrically fired Gatling-type gun, capable of firing anywhere from 3000 to 5000 rounds per minute. It was a devastating weapon, capable of causing a great deal of carnage and death.

Explosions rocked us. We could feel the concussions and the heat

1. First Encounter

from the rocket blasts almost a half a mile away. Ripples formed on the calm river waters. We saw the jungle burst into flames. Pieces of trees, shrubbery, and bamboo shot high into the air and dropped slowly back down, like the specks in a snow globe. We smelled smoke and burning meat. There was total devastation. The enemy stopped firing. They were dead. They had to be after that mind-boggling show of firepower.

That was the second day of my first trip up-river. We were cruising along, on our way to Moc Hoa, on the Vam Co Tay River, less than five "clicks" (kilometers) from Cambodia. Our mission was to deliver base

One of my crewmembers standing ready at the .50-caliber machine gun on the port side of our LCM-6. We had another one on the starboard side.

supplies to the Advanced Tactical Support Base (ATSB) that was the last outpost before the border. Those supplies consisted of food, beer, drinking water, and the ever-important toilet paper. In a fit of small rebellion, I had refused to carry barrels of gasoline in my boat. It just didn't make sense to me, as a boat captain, or as a human being with a brain, to carry highly flammable liquids in an area where there was a very good chance that they could be struck with hot bullets.

I considered the Mekong Delta to be the third most dangerous place for human beings in the year 1969. I ranked it slightly behind the moon, and Washington, D.C., where Richard Nixon was sworn in as president. The Mekong Delta was fifteen thousand square miles of wetlands and jungle and rivers (almost four times the size of the Everglades). The size of the area covered by water was determined by the season of the year. The area produced twenty million tons of rice and over three million tons of fish annually. It was interspersed with rice paddies, small villages, and well-hidden, heavily armed enemy combatants who wanted to kill me on a daily basis.

The U.S. Navy Mobile Riverine Force boats rarely traveled alone in the Delta. They generally traveled in groups, accompanied by varying numbers of the heavily armored Tango, Alpha, or Monitor boats (more on those later). Those boats carried larger crews, and bigger and more numerous weapons than we did on our fiberglass patrol boats or more lightly armored, but larger, supply boats. We never knew what the next turn would bring. Attacks were instantaneous and frenzied. We continually had to be on alert for an ambush and remained in a ready position whenever traveling those waterways. Flak jackets and helmets were the norm, but flak jackets were only minimally protective in that type of fighting. They provided decent protection from shrapnel and fragments from explosives and grenades, but did not offer a great deal of resistance to rifle and small arms fire. They did not protect your head or your extremities, only your chest and back. They were a sweat inducing burden in the stifling heat and humidity of the jungle. But they were a necessary burden if one wished to increase his chances of leaving Vietnam alive, with his body intact.

One minute we would be cruising down the river as if on a joy ride on Miami's Biscayne Bay, and the next minute the jungle would explode with the unmistakable sounds of AK-47 fire, .51-caliber machine gun fire, and the trailing smoke from B-40 rockets; often the attack came from both sides of the river, always chaotic.

After this first encounter with the enemy, I was mesmerized, in sort

1. First Encounter 7

This shows just how close I got to having my head blown off. That bullet hole missed my head by less than 24 inches and went through solid steel. That was from my first ambush on the river. (That's me at left.)

of a daze; a condition that seemed to overcome me on numerous occasions during my stay in Vietnam. I had just become a valid participant of war. I had popped my cherry. It wasn't just a newsreel anymore; it was live and in color, and scary as hell, and right in front of my face. I looked down; my pants were wet, and wet spots were very noticeable on solid green jungle fatigues. I wasn't the only one. Evidently bullets, explosions, and the threat of imminent death have an unnerving effect on one's bladder. It had all happened so fast; in a matter of seconds, really. While the bullets were flying, time slowed to a glacier's crawl. I heard the bullets ping against our boat and zip over our heads like buzzing bees. After I had calmed down slightly, and stopped shaking, I looked to my right and saw a bullet hole right through the armor plating near my head. I almost hyperventilated.

I just kept saying to myself, "Oh shit, oh shit, oh shit!!"

I also began to realize that I had probably just killed someone, or maybe even a number of people. I had taken the most precious gift of all. That was an utterly novel experience and a previously unvisited feeling for me. I immediately attempted to justify my actions to myself with the old "it was me or him" defense. After all, it was war, and that's what happened in war: people died. Still, the thought of killing someone, and the exponential effect that it had, was mind-boggling. I thought of his wife, kids, parents, nieces, nephews, friends ... they would all be affected by what I had just done, just as if the results had been reversed. Thoughts like those pursued me throughout my tour, after every firefight. Fortunately, because of the type of combat that I was involved in the majority of the time, I rarely had to look through the sights of my gun and witness the results of squeezing that trigger. It was almost always someone hidden in the jungle, someone I rarely saw, no one I ever made eye contact with. I had the luxury of deciding in my own mind that when they stopped shooting, they could either be dead or they had merely vacated the area. I had to convince myself that I had done nothing wrong, or else how could I live with it?

2

Go Back?

"Saigon ... shit!" Those were Martin Sheen's opening words in Francis Ford Coppola's epic Vietnam War classic, *Apocalypse Now*. Those words raced through my head as I made preparations to return to that forever, in my mind, memorable little corner of Southeast Asia. It had now been forty-two years since I blissfully departed there, and never in my wildest imagination did I ever think I would return. Seriously, who would want to? It was all that was amiss in the world at that time. It was the true epicenter of craziness and insanity, and a myriad of events that stretched the comprehending capabilities of one's mind. The memories of that tour arise still, on a regular basis. Not a day goes by, even after all those decades, that either some fleeting thought, or a very graphic representation of "that place," does not journey through my consciousness. Usually, it is for no more than a second or two, but more often than not, it morphs into a lingering awareness that brings forth sharp, pointed images of that part of my life. Images of circumstances and episodes that now seem genuinely bizarre, for no single event, or series of events in my life since then, has even come close to resembling anything that occurred back in that most peculiar life.

Don't get me wrong, though; there were positive aspects of that life experience. Much was ascertained there. I discovered things about the world, about people and their capabilities, but mostly about myself. It certainly was a time of discovery. Learning experiences encompassed chapters on personal limits, and how our individual upbringing and family-taught mores will, or won't, guide us during those times of difficult decision making. I learned how to deal with loss, horror, and revulsion, and how to make my mind acknowledge and accept the bizarre sights that my eyes were witnessing, no matter how repulsive. Things I learned there so many years ago have had more influence on the sort of person I am now than any other outside factor I have yet encountered. This is true even though, at this point in my life, it amounted to no more than a mere 2.3 percent of my total days on earth.

You see, the thing about being relegated into a situation such as war is that there is no other form of social interaction that compares to it in any way whatsoever. On those occasions when people ask the seemingly innocuous question, "What is war like?" what can I say? It is almost like sex in that respect because, in reality, it is comparable to nothing else you can encounter. One can compare it to no other experience; it is totally singular in "what it is like." Events took place during hostilities that could not occur under any other circumstances. Opportunities proffered themselves to individuals and groups that could never present themselves any place other than war. Decisions had to be made that would never arise during any other situation, both on a personal level and in a group dynamic. Those events, opportunities and decisions encompassed such questions and choices as whether or not to kill someone, whether or not to capture someone, whether or not to burn down a village, and whether or not to take advantage of a female captive. Those are things that just didn't arise on an everyday basis back home in Tennessee or Michigan or Miami Beach. Multitudes of decisions had to be made that meant life to some, and death to others. Those were choices that destroyed people's bodies, homes, fields, or futures. The choices that were ultimately opted for could, and did, separate or end family units and loved ones forever. Those decisions could make people love you, or hate you. That's a lot of responsibility for a 20-year-old Jewish kid from Miami. But those responsibilities were thrust upon countless young men, who up to that point in their lives had never had to make any decision more important than whom to ask to the prom.

Now, I found myself heading back there, to spend even more time in a setting that originally, and to this day, brought to mind thoughts as to what Dodge City must have been like in the mid–19th century. The Mekong Delta was a place where no one ever went anywhere unarmed, whether you were in a city, or a jungle, or a boat on the river. Prior to arriving in Vietnam, I had never even touched a gun. That was a venue where M-16s and side arms were as common as a crooked politician, or a sun visor in Miami. It was a place where the previously unencountered rumblings of gunfire or explosions had become no more than "white noise," akin to the sounds of traffic, or the buzz of overhead electric wires back home.

What made that entire situation even more bizarre, and certainly

2. Go Back?

surreal, was the fact that with all that going on, Saigon, and other small towns and villages that I happened upon in my journeys up and down the rivers, seemed to function in an almost normal manner. It was as if they were not really surrounded on all sides by horror and confusion and death. Unbelievably, amongst all this chaos and disorder, businesses were open, restaurants were feeding guests, and marketplaces were crowded. People were walking down the streets shopping. Women were dressed in beautiful ao dais (ow-yis), parading around as if it were Sunday afternoon in Omaha, Nebraska, or some other such nondescript place.

War was ravaging all around me. Death and destruction were rampant. Sights were totally alien to my still naive mind, and I just carried on wide-eyed, mouth agape, and unbelieving. Everyone was doing the best they could in this strange conglomeration of malevolence and confusion; it was all so surreal, so utterly freakish. I remember thinking of Kipling's famous, and oft repeated words, "If you can keep your head, when all about you/Are losing theirs and blaming it on you..." He must have foreseen the Mekong Delta in the 1960s, for that was what I had to do to survive the total absurdity and irrationality of the situation: literally just keep my head.

3

Flying Follies

So, now it's off to Miami International Airport to start this epic return journey. Our younger son drove, and as usual, the conversation evolved into a lively political discussion, since he's an ultra-conservative Republican, and my wife Mary and I are very liberal non-affiliates. Actually, we are lifestyle liberals, and financial conservatives. In spite of this, it always remained friendly and respectful, with no ill-will toward each other. There were many things in life we agreed upon, and only a few we didn't. We got along well and I always respected where he was coming from. He is a very intelligent and good-natured guy.

There was no traffic on the way, since it was Wednesday at noon, so the ride was uneventful as we pulled up to the new billion-dollar, graft-infused terminal at Miami International Airport. We checked in, and upon reaching the TSA security point, I detected one of life's true advantages to becoming a geezer. A very prominent sign stated that if you were born before this date in 1937, you were exempt from removing your shoes and sweater during the security section of your check-in. It's almost worth being seventy-five; I can't wait! And seriously, how many sweaters do you see in Miami? My wife and I dressed again, and headed for Gate D-4, which entailed a walk about the same distance as a half-marathon.

We stopped for lunch at Cu-Va, a Cuban restaurant in the terminal, where the food was two steps above mediocre. After lunch we headed to D-4 just in time to see, on the monitor, that our flight's gate had been changed to E-9. Before we made the lengthy journey to that gate, we tried to find out if that was really the case, as our boarding passes read differently. That is where we found out that the Yahoo! online article I read that concluded the rudest airline personnel in the world work for American Airlines was spot on. Even though I was first in line at the American counter, the overly helpful attendant kept ignoring me and helping people

3. *Flying Follies* 13

with a more, shall we say, Latino accent. Eventually, we found an attendant who reluctantly helped us and informed us that, sure enough, our gate had been changed and our flight was running about forty-five minutes late. We then rode the electric sidewalk to the intra-concourse train, to the escalators, and all this still left another half-marathon walk to the aforementioned E-9. But, as luck would have it, and as my ever-present positive karma stepped in, there was a bar at E-9, so this somewhat lessened the pain of overly rude flight attendants and epic walks. A cold beer can sometimes be a savior.

My first flight to Vietnam, in 1968, involved much less hassle, flying directly from Miami, after a thirty-day leave, to San Francisco. From there we traversed the Great Northern Route over Alaska, Japan, and finally on to Cam Ranh Bay, in the Republic of Vietnam. Cam Ranh Bay was a somewhat idyllic little spot in the middle of the maelstrom, with beautiful white beaches, surrounded by sand dunes and low-lying verdant rolling hills, jutting out into the South China Sea.

I don't remember any rude attendants (or as they were called then, stewardesses) on my initial flight to Southeast Asia. I only recall there being a great deal more apprehension, worry, and outright fear on the faces of everyone on that flight. Well, except for one guy I noticed across the aisle from me, who I am almost positive had dropped a tab of acid (LSD) somewhere over the North Pacific, judging by his freaky demeanor, his crazy eyes, and his ongoing conversations with himself.

I couldn't imagine the individual thoughts going on in each person's mind or how they each perceived what awaited them at the termination of that flight. I am certain that everyone had different visions and different expectations. I kept thinking to myself that a great adventure awaited me. I was certainly hoping for "adventure" over "debilitating experience." Thoughts of getting injured, or worse yet killed, never appeared. It just never entered my mind at that point, that war could have very serious consequences for the participants; maybe for some participants, but certainly not me. When you take your thoughts down from the overall picture, to the merely present and personal, very different thoughts and images result. Die? Me? Not a chance. This way of thinking was most likely the result of the many years of exposure to my mother's constant positive attitude. Her solution to most of life's problems and pitfalls was a stern, but knowing, "Just get over it, and move on!"

There was little talking amongst the passengers. A lot of introspection, I suspect, or maybe they all thought as I did: just one big adventure awaited us all. Of course, the termination of that flight would not involve any five-star hotels or a small luxurious river cruise ship inhabited by a hopefully friendly crew and gourmet chef. I also do not remember being graced with an exceedingly knowledgeable tour director, who knew the ins and outs of what I was to experience. The Navy just had guys who told you what needed to be done, and then they simply expected you to do it. In addition, I packed quite differently for this second trip, as the first trip did not require sandals, shorts, bathing suits, dress slacks, an as-yet uninvented laptop computer or iPhone, or very much money. There was no in-flight movie, just the incessant tediousness of a twenty-plus-hour flight, and the constant wondering of what it was going to be like. Images of daily newscasts and newspaper headlines floated through my head. I was quite confident that everyone's mindset on that flight was relatively different from what it would be on this new one. Yes, a very dissimilar trip so far.

In keeping with its renowned reputation as one of the world's premier people-unfriendly businesses, American Airlines, once again, did not disappoint us. After the trek to Gate E-9, we saw that the lighted, highly impersonal information board now informed us that our flight to San Francisco would be leaving from Gate D-34. We confirmed this, first with a gate attendant, who also told us the opposite of what our luggage check-in person told us: we would not have to retrieve our luggage in San Francisco before checking in to our flight on Cathay Pacific. Our luggage had been checked all the way to Saigon ... excuse me, Ho Chi Minh City. Let us not forget who actually won that war, and by so doing, reserved the right to change the name of anything they wanted. Our luggage check-in guy, in Miami, was quite adamant about our retrieving our luggage in San Francisco. Those American Airlines people couldn't even agree with each other. We did yet another half-marathon back to D-34, and waited.

Finally, after an additional half-hour delay, we departed Miami almost an hour and a half after our scheduled departure time. With the exception of the evil little boy sitting directly behind me, and directly in front of Mary, since American could not see fit to seat my wife and me together, the flight was uneventful, and uneventful is always a good thing when flying. That kid never shut up. He whined and moaned and kicked seats all the way across America.

We arrived in San Francisco an hour and a half late and hurried through the terminal where we asked an information officer how to get to Cathay Pacific. He told us to go up the elevator and catch the train to the International Terminal. We stopped first, though, at the American Airlines counter to confirm that we did not have to claim our luggage. We did not, but the American Airlines rep told us that it was faster to walk

3. Flying Follies

to the International Terminal than to take the train. Again we were steered wrong by American representatives, and ended up doing one last half-marathon. Would I never learn? Was American Airlines just messing with Mary and me? Fortunately, the entire flying experience transformed for the better the instant we encountered our first Cathay Pacific representative. He was friendly, courteous, knowledgeable, and expedient. We checked in, received boarding passes, and spent twenty minutes getting through security, ending up at gate A-3, with thirteen minutes to spare before boarding.

The Boeing 777 was a magnificent plane. Our seats were just about amidships in row forty-four of eighty. Mary got her usual window seat, and I got my usual aisle seat, with a gentleman from Bangladesh between us. This was my first encounter with a Bangladeshi. He explained to us that he had a twelve-hour layover in Hong Kong before he could fly home; poor guy. We received our menus and prepared for dinner, then a movie, then hopefully some sleep, before breakfast on this fourteen-hour flight.

There was no menu on my previous flight to Vietnam, way back then, but we were given a choice of assorted sandwiches, and by assorted I mean either roast beef or roast beef with lettuce, and canned sodas. As I vaguely recall, the sandwiches were almost tasty, and relatively fresh. There was no in-flight movie, and there were certainly no attractive, attentive, Asian flight attendants tending to our needs. World Airways was about as utilitarian as any airline could be. It was the Yugo of airlines. How fortunate that I didn't have to pay anything for that flight. What there was, though, was plenty of free alcoholic drinks for those who wanted to toss back a few; those who wanted to forget about where they were headed. A few imbibed, but most did not. That flight held only ninety passengers, as opposed to this flight that carried over three hundred, and all ninety of us had varying thoughts. Those thoughts were about getting there, and our chances of returning one day to our homes. There were thoughts about what it would be like; thoughts about how we would act, and react. Thoughts about whether we would make our flights home afterwards in a seat ... or in a box.

At that time Vietnam was daily news. It was a dark room, full of deadly objects. A faraway place as completely removed from reality as Baghdad, Iwo Jima, Guadalcanal, the Argonne Forest or Gettysburg must have seemed to the men who ended up in those places, in their wars, in their day. Death counts were presented every day, like baseball scores, both the enemy's and our own. Everyone knew someone who had gone to Vietnam and not returned, or had returned in a very dissimilar condition from when they had departed home. Certainly no one returned as the same person who had left the good old USA. Vietnam was a place of flux for everyone who ended up there. It profoundly changed every person who experienced it ... some mentally, some physically, but everyone was changed, in one way or another, when he left there. Everyone had stories. Everyone had memories of things he was either proud of, or things he was not so proud of; the things that nightmares are made of. Recollections better lost from memory altogether.

4.

Hong Kong to Saigon

I must say at this point that Cathay Pacific knows how to run an airline, and how to treat people. All the personnel we came in contact with were just like that first guy I mentioned: pleasant, knowledgeable, and efficient. The 14-hour flight from San Francisco to Hong Kong was loaded with movie, TV, and game options on the seat-back screens, and all of the meals were served with minimum hassle. The quality of the food was excellent, in most instances, for airline food, and the attendants were always there when needed, and always in a pleasant and helpful mood. Remind me to write a letter to Cathay Pacific commending them on a job well done. We arrived in Hong Kong at 5:30 a.m. local time. It was a beautiful morning. We checked through security and headed for Gate-27 for our final flight ... to Ho Chi Minh City. We enjoyed a latte in the terminal coffee shop, after which we charged our phones and laptop computer.

As is the norm for Cathay Pacific, our flight to Saigon departed right on schedule. The weather was gorgeous, but as we all know, traveling is always a learning experience. For instance, on this particular flight I learned to never, and I repeat, never order anything that ends with the word "congee." Turns out that "beef congee," which I opted for instead of the omelet with hash browns and sausage, turned out to be 2 slices of beef approximately the size of a quarter, in a good 6–8 ounces of what the attendant described as "porridge." But this was such a vile-tasting and soupy-textured porridge that had Charles Dickens known about it, Oliver Twist would never have asked for "more, please!" and the whole story line would have changed. After the "Congee Incident," the rest of the flight was par for the course. We flew into Saigon over the Mekong Delta. "The Mekong Delta" ... words and a sight that brought up such distant memories.

Without asking, the coffee shop in the Hong Kong airport welcomed us at 5 a.m. with their artistic version of a morning wake-up latte.

We landed at Tan San Nhut airport, in the midst of this ten-million-person megalopolis. In the late sixties, Tan San Nhut was the busiest airport in the entire world.

5

HOW THE NAVY GOT ME TO VIETNAM

Getting to Vietnam the first time involved a much more convoluted and circuitous journey than going as a tourist. The Navy didn't immediately send me to Vietnam after I completed boot camp. Prior to arriving there in 1969, I had already served for almost a year and a half.

My enlistment began at the induction center in Coral Gables, Florida. On the day I was scheduled to leave for Navy boot camp, the center was in chaos. It was pure craziness. That was 1967, and there were protests against the war, there was a draft, and no one wanted to go. There were guys who had already been drafted and scheduled to leave but were still trying to get out of going. Some were dressed as women, and there were guys kissing other guys (which, in those days, was somewhat unusual). There were men acting mentally deranged, showing signs of uncontrolled spasms or tics in numerous parts of their bodies. There were guys on crutches with fake casts on their legs or arms. One guy showed up naked. There were young men who did a multitude of drugs or drank a half gallon of coffee before showing up so that their initial physicals would show abnormalities in their results, and hopefully disqualify them. Some brought their mothers in to beg the Army not to take their "little boys." It was sad, but the entertainment value alone was worth my enlistment. It was like visitor day at an insane asylum. There were hundreds of draftees present that day and none of them wanted to be there.

Out of the hundreds present, only four of us were scheduled to go into the Navy and we were enlistees. All the others were Army draftees and a few unfortunates who were actually drafted into the Marine Corps. You had to have really bad karma to be drafted into the Marines. We four were met by a Navy lieutenant who treated us like human beings. He was cordial, proper, and to the point. He told us that because we had enlisted, and not been drafted, we were to be afforded certain special privileges. It was February, and the lieutenant told us that one of those special privileges was that we would have our choice as to where to go to boot camp. At that time the Navy had two boot camps, one in Chicago and one in San Diego. We all looked at each other, smiled, and in unison, as if it had been rehearsed, told the lieutenant that San Diego would be just fine. He made the arrangements and a few hours later we were airborne on a Delta flight heading west.

When we landed and got off the plane, we thought that the lieutenant had surely played some kind of horrific joke on us. It was thirty-one degrees, and we believed we had been sent to Chicago. As it turned out, it was San Diego, but not quite the San Diego we had all envisioned.

Boot camp ended up being interesting, as well as informative. After the initial shock of being in the military and being treated as the scum of the earth, it got better. One of my favorite events was our first military haircut. Remember, this was the sixties, and many recruits showed up with afros, or hair down to their shoulders, or even longer. When I sat in the chair for my haircut, the barber asked me nonchalantly whether I wanted my sideburns or not. I naively told him that I did. He then ran his clippers up the side of my head and said, "Here, catch 'em!" and then laughed uproariously. I had no doubt that I was the thousandth guy that had fallen for that, and he still got a kick out of it. He was a funny guy, or at least he thought so.

Navy boot camp was not like the Army or Marines, where they stressed physicality, fighting, and other combat situations. We spent about half of every day in classrooms, and the other half doing on-the-job training. We learned about ships, the sea, knots, firefighting, weather, boat handling and a myriad of other things that would actually be useful in real life, after we left the military. We also learned to march, which seemed inane to me, as Navy men never marched anywhere except in boot camp. I guessed that it was kind of a discipline thing.

My training company (#126) was comprised mostly of guys from Oklahoma, Oregon, Kansas, and some of the Southern states; almost all of them were rednecks and country boys. We even had a guy from Alabama whose first name was just the letter R. I assumed that his family had spelling issues. I was named company yeoman, or clerk. I took notes, did all the writing, filled out reports for the company commander, and followed the inspectors around as they inspected the troops. I got that job because I had legible handwriting, and I knew how to type, thanks to the

5. How the Navy Got Me to Vietnam

one semester I took in high school as an elective. Boot camp lasted 12 weeks, and it was one of the best practical learning experiences I have ever had.

After graduating boot camp I was sent to basic electronics and electricity school, at Treasure Island in San Francisco, but not for long. I didn't like it, and I was itching to get into the "real" Navy. I soon got my wish. I quit the electronics school and two weeks later got orders to join the "fleet." I was assigned to the USS *Banner*, AGER-1, whose home port was Yokosuka, Japan. I was excited, but when I went to do research on exactly what an "AGER" was, I found no info on it. No one on the base knew what kind of ship it was or what it did. I finally found out that "AGER" was a designation for "experimental research ship," but no one could tell me precisely what its function was.

I flew to Japan in September of 1967 via the Great Northern Route, with a stopover in Fairbanks, Alaska. We had a three-hour layover and were told to wait in the terminal. As I walked down the stairway from the plane to the tarmac my fingers froze solid to the handrail and an attendant had to pour hot water down the railing to free me. That was my first encounter with snow and ice in my life. Eventually I made it to Tachikawa, Japan, and was met by a Navy driver who drove me the fifty miles to the Yokosuka Naval Base. The *Banner* was not there. She was out on operations. I stayed in the enlisted bachelor quarters for ten days, shooting pool and wandering around town, waiting for her to return.

When she did arrive, and I saw her, I was devastated. She was the second smallest (182 feet) oceangoing ship in the Navy, was a leftover from World War II, had a crew of sixty-two, and was ugly. I was assigned to the deck crew, which meant maintenance while in port, and lookout watches and helm watches while at sea. It was a very un-military ship. We could grow beards if we wanted, as long as you grew it out at sea, and it was not scraggly looking by the time we got back to home port. No one on the ship knew how to operate the anchor. The radar system worked only intermittently. We had two civilian oceanographers aboard to make it look like we were

The uniform patch from the USS *Banner* AGER-1, sister ship of the USS *Pueblo* AGER-2. We were home ported in Yokosuka, Japan.

really an oceanographic research ship. The Russians and Chinese knew better, though, and followed us closely when we operated near their coasts.

Most of the ship's personnel were made up of communication technicians (CTs). Those were very strange guys who spoke Russian, Chinese, and Korean. The ones that weren't interpreters were techies. "Techies" was not a word used in the sixties, but that's what they were: specialty electronics experts. The CTs were not part of the ship's crew; they were a separate entity. They were not involved in the running of the ship, nor did they have to perform any of the normal duties aboard her. They had their own secret spaces, and the ship's real crew was made up of only about 25 of us. That was not what I had in mind when I thought of Navy ships and what I had hoped to do in the Navy.

We left Yokosuka six days later. That was when I found out exactly what the *Banner* did. She was an electronics listening ship, or more commonly, a "spy" ship. We headed north from Yokosuka, through the Tsugaru Straits, a channel between Honshu and Hokkaido in northern Japan, then west-southwest across the Sea of Japan. We ended up in an area that was twelve to fifteen miles off the coast of Vladivostok, Siberia, on the southern tip of the Muravyov-Amursky Peninsula. We were covertly listening to the Russians. The weather was terrible. I had never experienced anything like it in my life. When we arrived at our area of operations, it was forty degrees below zero, with a thirty-knot wind and twenty-foot seas. I was sick as a dog. The second day there, I was on the helm, and the captain entered the bridge.

I asked him, "Sir, could I speak with you for a second?"

He said, "Sure, what is it?"

I said, "Sir, I'm from Miami, I really shouldn't be here."

He just looked at me kind of funny and walked away shaking his head. After that, I hated it even more. I knew I was stuck on that ship for a while. We stayed there for thirty days before heading back to Yokosuka. I lost twenty pounds.

Back in Yokosuka, it took me a full day of walking on dry land to get rid of the motion sickness. For hours, it was as if I was still out at sea: my legs unsure, my head spinning, a feeling of nausea permeating my consciousness. I went into town every night while in port for a few drinks and a few hook-ups with some very sociable young Japanese women. It took our entire in-port time for me to recuperate fully.

Six days later we left Yokosuka again, but this time we headed south, into the Yellow Sea, off the coast of China to listen in on the Chinese for a while. On the way, we stopped for a couple of nights in Sasebo, Japan.

5. How the Navy Got Me to Vietnam

Sasebo's claim to fame was that it was home to Tokyo Rose during World War II. She broadcast her anti–American sentiments from a studio set up in the mountains surrounding the huge port and shipbuilding center of Sasebo.

Upon arriving at our area of operations, off the Chinese Coast, it was over one hundred degrees and the seas were mirror-like. It reminds me of that Americas' song, "A Horse with No Name" about the sea being "a desert with its life underground and the perfect disguise above." In a matter of one and a half weeks I had gone through a one hundred and forty degree temperature change. That operating schedule went on until January of 1968, when our sister ship, the USS *Pueblo*, AGER-2, was captured by the North Koreans. The ship and crew were taken hostage into Wonsan, where they were kept and abused for a year. After sitting off the coast of Korea for three weeks with an entire task force of twenty ships, the *Banner* returned to Yokosuka and was never sent out again. The *Pueblo* was never released. We had become obsolete now that the North Koreans had access to all of our electronics.

6

JAPAN AND OVERT SEXUALITY

Living in Japan for a year, while stationed on the USS *Banner*, was a bizarre as well as surprising experience. After growing up in Miami, and spending summers in Boston, I had no idea as to how the rest of the world worked or operated, what the day-to-day lives of foreigners comprised, and how it differed from my own life experiences. I had never been outside the United States, so my frame of reference for how the peoples of the world lived was limited to the east coast of America. "Join the Navy and See the World" was one of the reasons I enlisted and, in all probability, the motive for many other young men who had joined the Navy and wished to familiarize themselves with and experience other cultures.

I was fully aware of the various differences within the confines of my own country, as I experienced the oddities (or what I perceived as oddities) of the people of New England. I spent every summer of my life, from birth to the age of seventeen, in Nantasket, a small, beautiful, quaint oceanfront town on the south shore of Boston, in my family's beach house. The distinct accent was the most obvious of their dissimilarities with South Floridians, but it went further than just the accents. They had different names for everyday products and services that I had thought were universal in the USA. What I knew as Coke, or just plain soda, they referred to as "tonic," and they said "grinder" instead of a sub sandwich, "dropped eggs" instead of poached eggs, a "bubbler" instead of a water fountain, a "frappe" instead of a milkshake, and numerous other things I had to learn to survive as a summer kid in New England.

Japan was like New England on steroids as far as social differences and expected norms. Besides the obvious things, like driving on the left side of the road, different money, smells, foods, and architecture, there was the incomprehensible language barrier, both spoken and the written word. It was soon after I arrived that I discovered another most glaring difference. I had never been subject to the concept of "bar girls," or "hostesses." I never hung out in bars because back then, one had to be twenty-one to drink in Florida and Massachusetts, but in the Japan of the 1960s, they rarely checked IDs.

Hostesses were any of the thousands of young ladies who plied their trade in the bars in the Navy ports of Yokosuka and Sasebo, as well as other military ports and towns throughout the Pacific, and I imagine, the rest of the world. They were there for two reasons. Firstly, to make sure that everyone who entered any particular bar stayed for an extended period, and bought numerous alcoholic drinks. Secondly, the hostesses were compelled to urge the visitors to purchase drinks for them as well. Even though the hostess's drinks cost the same, or sometimes even more than the patrons', they normally consisted of tea instead of liquor (tea looks just like bourbon or whiskey), even though they were served in the same shot or mixed-drink glasses. To me, this was fully understandable, as I could plainly see what the effects would be for any of the women if they had to partake of real alcoholic drinks every night in the numbers that they consumed. The more drinks the sailor bought the young lady, the longer she would stay with him at his table and give the illusion that she wanted to be there.

In addition to the aforementioned duties of the "escort/hostesses," there was the underlying aspect of the possibility of sexual favors. Bear in mind that in a port, such as Yokosuka, Sasebo, Naha, Hong Kong, or Subic Bay, there were approximately two hundred bars within walking distance of the base gate. Each bar had a minimum of five to seven hostesses working inside, which meant that at any given time there were over a thousand "escort/hostesses" available for negotiations. I don't know how the "sexual favor" aspect worked with the ladies, in terms of what their split with the house was, or what specific rules guided their behavior. What was obvious was that sex was available for the right price, and was being promoted by the establishments in a very overt manner. Business cards were distributed throughout the city, as well as on the military bases, offering differing services, but all with sexually explicit overtones. As is plainly seen from the cards I saved, everything from naked beauties to "stem" baths, to much "engoyment," to "full-bosomed eager young hostesses," to blatant offers of intercourse, was offered to anyone who cared to partake.

This was a whole new slant (no pun intended) on my previously perceived idea of acceptable social interaction. I had never seen sex advertised on business cards before, as if they were advertising a game room, or something similar. It did make the nights interesting, but bear in mind

WELCOME TO
BAR CHARLIE'S

CHEAP & MUCH ENJOYMENT IN THIS BAR
NAKED BEAUTY SERVES YOU
INTRCOURSE IF YOU WANT
STEM-BATH MASSAGE & RUBDOWN

5-5 TOKIWA-CHO SASEBO
TEL. (2) 2369

WELCOME
BAR NIGHT TRAIN
"YOUR NO FISH IF YOU DIG THIS"

CHEAP & MUCH ENJOYMENT IN THIS
BAR.
HOURS. ALSO HONEST, PRETTY GIRLS
WILL SERVE YOU UNTILL YOU GET
SATISFACTION......GIVE USA TRY. !!

5-15 SAKAE-MACHI SASEBO
TEL. 3-0574

Welcome to the cozy bar

BAR PEARL
in Ginza

Behind of Tokyo U.S.O.

Plenty of wine &
charming hostesses

Open 10:00 a.m. to 11:00 p.m.

Tel: 561-4060

4, 3-chome, Ginza,
Chuo-ku, Tokyo

For Taxi Driver:

BAR TWILIGHT
AREN,T YOU INTERESTED ?

CHEAP AND MUCH ENGOYMEN,T IN OUR PLACE.
NAKED BEAUTY SERYES YOU, INTERCOURSE
IF YOU WANT. STEAMBATH, RUBDOWN AND
MASSAGE

BAR WEST COAST

YOU DON'T NEED BUY FOR GIRL

STEAM BATH MASSAGE.
AND NAKED BEAUTY ?
SKIN SHOW

6—3 TOKIWA-MACHI SASEBO PARADISE ST.

WELCOME
BAR KITTYCAT

YOU WILL BE SATISFIED WITH OUR
BEATIFUL GIRL'S AND CHEAP DRINKS
VERY GOOD SERVICE AND FREE
DRINKS PLEASE CONE WE APPRE
CIATE YOUR BUSINESS
THANK YOU VERYMUCH

IF YOU WANT STEAMBATH AND MASSAGE
5-5 TOKIWA-CHO SASEBO

GIRLS! GIRLS! GIRLS!
GUARANTEED BEAUTIFUL
FULL-BOSOMED, EAGER YOUNG
HOSTESSES READY TO SOOTHE YOUR
NEEDS

RELAX, ENJOY YOURSELF
WE AIM TO PLEASE

WELCOME
CLUB SASEBO

#7-6 TOKIWA-MACHI SASEBO PARADISE ST.

Cards used to entice military and visitors into specific bars and clubs in Sasebo, Japan ... usually promising things they did not deliver.

6. Japan and Overt Sexuality

Me, standing outside one of the many bars in Sasebo, Japan, in full dress blues, while on liberty.

that the main function of the bar ladies was to sell drinks, as many drinks as they possibly could, both for the patron and for themselves. That was the business that sustained the bars, and the women were very good at pushing those drinks, as well as flirting. As far as I could tell, there was very little actual sex going on, merely the promise and illusion of possible sex. More often than not, in the majority of cases, the end result was that the sailor had spent all of his money on drinks for himself and his lady friend, and had none left for the carnal delights that were so openly promised throughout the night's encounter in the bars.

7

SUBIC BAY, DIVING AND CORONADO

After the *Pueblo* incident, I asked for a transfer off the *Banner*, and out of the Land of the Rising Sun. I was tired and bored with sitting in Japan, and besides, it was expensive. Finances didn't matter when I was only in port for six days out of thirty, but now that we were permanently tied up in Yokosuka, each of my meager paychecks could not last until the next one. It took time to get transferred in the Navy, unless it was their idea. In September, the ship's yeoman informed me that he had gotten a bulletin from the Naval Bureau of Personnel (BUPERS) stating that the Navy was looking for volunteers to become divers. I volunteered on the spot. The only problem was that the class started in one week, in Subic Bay, Philippines, at the U.S. Navy Dive School, and I was in Japan. There wasn't enough time, through proper channels, for me to get transfer orders. The executive officer of the *Banner* offered to help me. He had fake orders drawn up, but told me that when and if I graduated from dive school there would be no further orders awaiting me, as BUPERS would not know that I was in the Philippines. I had to swear to him that I would never mention his name in regards as to how I got there. He said the dive school people could worry about the problem, when and if I graduated, and they could work it out.

With the help, once again, from the executive officer of the *Banner*, I got a flight almost immediately to the Philippines, on a military air command (MAC) plane out of Tachikawa, and reported to naval dive school, Subic Bay Naval Ship Repair Facility (SRF). I gave them a copy of my orders (which evidently looked real enough to them) and was assigned living quarters. That school and training turned out to be the most difficult twelve weeks of my life up to that point, but I ended up in the best shape

7. Subic Bay, Diving and Coronado

I had ever been in. They made us run and swim for hours every day, building up our stamina and leg strength. We swam on our backs in the pool, wearing twin scuba tanks and fins for two hours every morning. That was after running five miles. Leg cramps became the norm. We had to swim laps in the pool while holding a towel in each hand, and towels got very heavy when wet. There were classes in scuba diving, hard hat diving (deep sea suits), and "Jack Brown," or shallow water diving. "Jack Brown" diving consisted of wearing a full face mask which had an air hose connected to a topside air compressor. It was good for depths up to thirty-three feet, and made shallow-water dive work much easier because of the lack of tanks and regulators. It was usually used when working on ship hulls. We had to actually drown in school. We were required to lie in the bottom of the pool until we passed out, then brought to the surface and revived by one of our classmates. It was a very difficult thing to do. Your body just does not want to drown.

Learning to function in the deep sea suit was the most difficult phase of the school to endure. It was heavy and cumbersome. It took two additional people to help the diver get dressed and undressed, and the suit was very confining. The helmet and breastplate weighed thirty-seven pounds. The canvas suit weighed twenty pounds. The weight belt was eighty-four pounds, and the shoes weighed in at fifty-six pounds. It was usually warm in the suit and peripheral vision was greatly hindered because of limited movement options. The gloves were clumsy and made some jobs very difficult.

My most frightening experience occurred while in a deep sea diving suit. I was in sixty-five feet of water. The dive helmet contained a radio and a mouth-controlled valve that could manipulate the amount of air that was released from or retained within the suit. Many times you needed to retain air in the dive suit so that you could achieve neutral buoyancy. That was important when walking on soft mud or silty sea bottoms, as those suits weighed almost two hundred pounds with no one in them. As I pulled the valve with my teeth to retain some air in the suit, and reach that state of neutral buoyancy, the elbow patch blew out. My suit began to fill with water and mud through the resulting hole. I slowly sank over my head into the soft bottom mud and only then realized why the first thing the Navy did when one started dive school was to test each prospective diver for claustrophobia. I radioed the tender and let him know about my situation. I knew, from my training, that the water in the suit could not rise up into my helmet, unless I turned upside down, because of the air pressure inside the helmet. They eventually had to bring a floating crane with a platform, and send down two more divers, to get me topside. I weighed over 700 pounds at that point, which included my own weight of one hundred sixty pounds, the dive suit, and almost four hundred pounds of mud and water. They said that when I broke the surface on the platform, I resembled a fountain, with water and mud shooting out of the elbow hole.

After the second week of school, we were allowed off base, into the city of Olongapo, which was made up of hotels, bars, and women. That was it; hundreds of each. No one had the energy to leave the base for the first two weeks anyway. We were all so tired and sore each night following school that most of us fell asleep right after the evening meal. After learning my way around Olongapo, I met some interesting people. OK, I met some interesting women, and the following week, I rented an apartment six blocks from the base. The cost was sixteen dollars a month, which included running water, electricity, and two young women: Remedios and

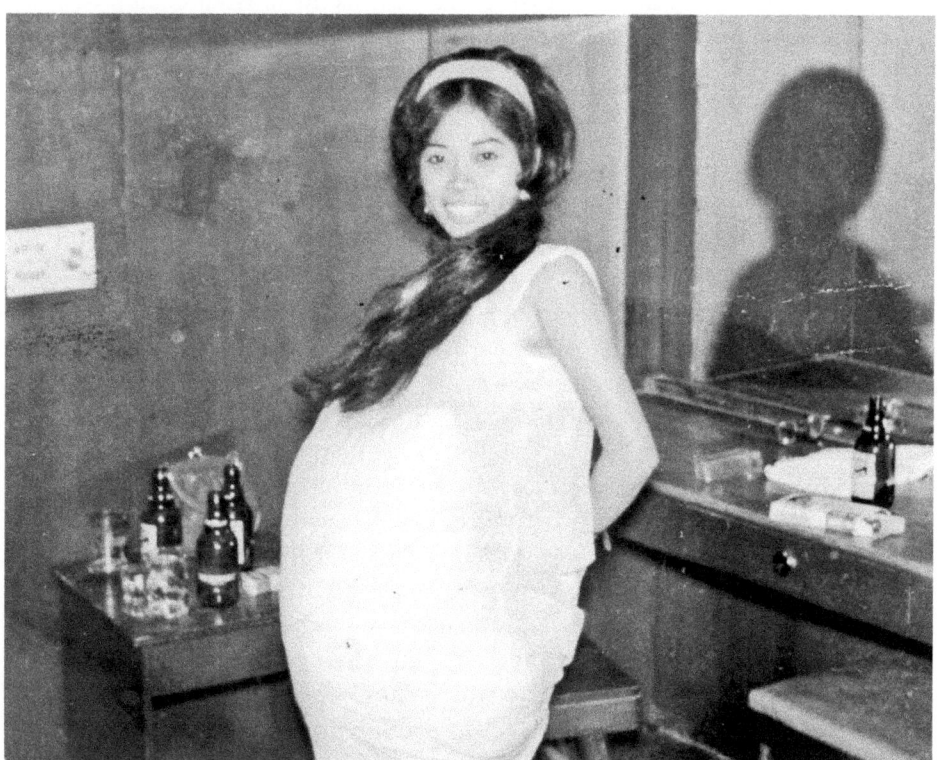

My roommate, Remedios, in Subic Bay, while attending Dive School, playing a joke on me.

7. Subic Bay, Diving and Coronado

her cousin, Leonora. They were both very nice, had great senses of humor and were a definite "ten" on the entertainment scale. Living with those two women had advantages over and above the obvious, though. They did the food shopping and the cooking, which was far superior to the mess hall food on the base, and they kept our small two-story townhouse apartment clean and neat. The apartment had a living room, dinette, and kitchen on the first floor, and a bathroom and one bedroom on the second floor. That living arrangement made the school more than bearable for the next ten weeks. When I did have to leave the Philippines, I pre-paid the rent on the apartment for an entire year ($192) so that they would have a nice place to live. They were very grateful.

My other roommate, Remedios's cousin Leonora. They were great cooks, and supplied over-the-top companionship.

After the twelve weeks, during which I became proficient at all types of underwater tasks, I was one of only four men who completed the course and graduated. That was out of a starting class of sixteen. I learned how to weld underwater, as well as search techniques, recovery techniques, and small demolition jobs using C-4 plastic explosives. C-4 was a malleable explosive material which could be formed into almost any shape and set off with a detonator and detonator cord. We used the explosives for two main purposes. We used it to help blow propellers off their shafts on small boats when they needed to be replaced. This method was substantially easier than using a heavy hammer underwater to try to pound it off. The other reason we learned to use

C-4 was to blow up sunken boats that were impeding river traffic in Vietnam. You just place the explosive in numerous spots around the sunken boat, attach primer cord, and then, most importantly, get out of the water before detonating. I experienced being in the water during an explosion and it felt exactly like a huge electric shock. If you are too close to an underwater explosion it can blow out your insides.

In the picture below, notice the double-hosed regulator I was wearing. Single-hose regulators, which are now the norm, were just coming into use at that time, but were not available in aluminum. Those of us who dove in Vietnam were limited to using aluminum tanks and regulators because we were going to be diving in waters where magnetic mines were in use and aluminum would not set them off, as would steel, if we came in contact with them. Upon graduation I was given a certificate of designation and awarded the honor of wearing the Navy Diver's emblem on my dress uniform, and later on my jungle fatigues in Vietnam. That showed that I was a certified and designated Navy Diver. I was very proud of that designation, as the Navy was always seeking volunteers to attend dive school, but few qualified, and even fewer managed to complete the course. I had qualified in all aspects, except that my eyesight was not quite what was required by the Navy. That was overlooked at the time, because of the Navy's need for divers, and I was supplied with a prescription face mask, made by Navy opticians.

That little emblem under the diver's emblem on my dress uniform was given to me because I also qualified as an anti-aircraft machine gunner. I was trained on 20MM anti-aircraft cannons at a special school on the other side of the base. Bear in mind, though, that I was a qualified anti-aircraft machine gunner in a war where the enemy had

That's me waving to the cameraman underwater in Cam Ranh Bay, while installing an underwater lighting system around the dock area, in order to see any enemy swimmers who may enter the area at night.

7. Subic Bay, Diving and Coronado

This is the document showing my successful completion of the twelve-week-long U.S. Navy Dive school in Subic Bay, Philippines.

no planes. Yes, I know, I also wondered about that designation and seemingly wasted training.

Upon graduating from dive school, I received no further orders. Everyone was surprised but me. The other three graduates were all heading in different directions. One was headed for a sub-tender (a submarine maintenance ship); one was headed for a repair facility in Long Beach, California; and the third guy got orders to Da Nang, Vietnam as a repair diver. The *Banner*'s executive officer was right: the Bureau of Personnel didn't know I was there. They thought that I was still aboard the *Banner*. The school officials merely thought that there was some type of paperwork mix-up, and put in for new orders, forwarding BUPERS a copy of my graduation papers from dive school.

While awaiting orders, I was assigned to the dive locker as a base diver. I ended up doing over 20 dives while my orders were being drawn up. I repaired a leak in the hull of a sinking tugboat by welding a steel plate over the hole. I recovered a young child's body from the canal that

Left: My dress blue uniform patches designating my qualifications as a U.S. Navy Diver as well as a qualified antiaircraft machine gunner. *Right:* My diver designation patch on my jungle fatigues in Vietnam. Divers were a small group of elite Navy specialists. Strictly voluntary duty.

separated the base from the city of Olongapo. What a very depressing day that turned out to be. We made dives to some of the sunken ships in the harbor, a number of which had been there since World War II. Diving in Subic was a good experience, as it was very clean, clear water, and I was involved in a multitude of different types of dives. It was a good learning experience. I also taught a platoon of recon (reconnaissance patrol) Marines how to tie a bowline knot. Recon Marines were a special ops group that performed "unconventional special operations" in support of "conventional" warfare. Because of their various methods of airborne, helicopter, submarine, and waterborne insertions and extractions, it was necessary for them to learn how to utilize scuba gear. The recon Marines were sent to the school only for the scuba part of the training. Tying knots and performing minor underwater work tasks was part of that training.

Only one dive caused problems. The USS *Long Beach* (CGN-9), a nuclear-powered guided missile cruiser, was in port and needed new zinc plates welded to the hull in a hurry so that she could be back "on-line" off the coast of Vietnam. All ships had zinc plates attached to their hulls. Those plates helped prevent electrolytic corrosion to the steel of the ship

7. Subic Bay, Diving and Coronado

by attracting the electrolytes from the sea water, which allowed the plates to rust and dissipate, instead of the steel hulls. It was basically a corrosion protection system.

We were set up into three-man teams, each team working two four-hour shifts a day. There was one man standing watch, one man holding the zinc plate in place under the hull, and one man spot welding the plate to the hull. Besides the welding equipment, we had a five-hundred-watt light to illuminate the work area, a suction cup handle attached to the hull so that we could gain leverage while holding the eight-pound plate in place, and a watch diver brandishing a bang stick. A bang stick was an eight- to ten-foot-long pole with a twelve-gauge shotgun shell attached at one end that could be fired by pressing it against any solid target. One of our shifts was from midnight to four a.m. Around two a.m., the watch tapped my shoulder and pointed. I looked to where he was pointing and saw a huge gray shadow slowly swimming in a circle around us. It was a twelve- to fourteen-foot great white shark, a somewhat common sight in Subic Bay. Its circle was getting smaller as it continued swimming. I tapped the welder on the shoulder and made him aware of our visitor. He looked at me and pointed up. That was diver jargon for, and once again I am paraphrasing here, "Get the hell out of the water, now!" He dropped his welding gear to the bottom, about fifteen feet below us. I dropped the zinc plate that was being readied to be attached, and we swam parallel to the hull until we reached the edge of the ship, and headed upward as quickly as we could. The shark followed. He got within about six feet of the watch, who then extended his bang stick and hit the shark just below his snout. The shotgun shell exploded in an array of shark skin and blood. It did not kill the shark, but it did piss him off and distract him long enough for us to make the last forty feet to the surface and climb aboard the dive barge. We looked like orca-chased penguins leaping out of the water onto an ice floe. We didn't go back down to finish our shift in the now bloody water, but when it got light, the next group of divers showed up and did their stint. We had learned in school that sharks normally fed at night and were attracted by light. I did as little night diving as possible after that close encounter.

Finally, my new orders arrived, in the form of instructions for me to report to the Inshore Undersea Warfare Group (IUWG) at Coronado Island, California. I left for California two days later and arrived in Coronado, near San Diego. There were no open beds for me at the base, so the Navy put me up at the Hotel Del Coronado, one of the few times—no, the only time I had maid and room service paid for by the Navy. The school consisted of classroom training in harbor control techniques. I stayed for two weeks and then got my orders to Cam Ranh Bay, Vietnam, and Inshore Undersea Warfare Group #1.

I then went home on a thirty-day leave, where I spent twenty-eight of those days with a young lady that one of my sisters introduced me to. We had a wonderful time together. It had always been a real positive thing to have sisters. Our house was continuously full of their female friends and acquaintances, and on many occasions, a number of them became my special friend and acquaintance. My friends also came around to visit when I was home. None of them had made it into the military, some because of physical reasons and some due to mental shortcomings. Back then, you could actually take classes on how to beat the draft and how to create enough doubt within the heads of the military psychiatrists or psychologists so that they would deem you unfit for military service. One of those reports about one of my good friends (who shall remain nameless) from the Army psychiatrist actually went a step further, stating, "I find this young man unfit for military service ... or anything else." Another friend took me aside and told me that he never expected to see me again because he was sure: "You won't make it back, Richie." With

A copy of the Geneva Convention card carried by all U.S. military personnel, even though North Vietnam was never a signer of the Geneva Convention.

7. Subic Bay, Diving and Coronado

this bit of positive attitude, my leave came to an end and I flew to California.

I was sent to Survival, Escape, Resistance, and Evasion (SERE) training (see Chapter 8), and upon completion was issued a Geneva Convention ID card, even though North Vietnam was never a signer of the Geneva Convention. I didn't learn that little tidbit of information until after the war, though, and I certainly would have been mighty miffed to find out, upon being captured, that I was not going to be treated well. It's not a good thing in war, if only one of the sides adheres to certain predetermined humanitarian rules, and the other side does not. My next flight was to Cam Ranh Bay.

8

Prep-Work for War

In 1969, before deploying to Vietnam, it was mandatory that all military personnel go through Survival, Escape, Resistance, and Evasion (SERE) training. For Naval personnel, that training took place in Warner Springs, California, located in the midst of the 560,000-acre Cleveland National Forest. The training and education facility was located in the mountains, at an elevation of about 3,200 feet, inland of the coast, and almost due east of San Diego. It was cold, it was barren, and it was isolated. We had to forage for food, learn to read topographical maps, determine how to procure water, and shelter ourselves during the cold nights. Each person was supplied with a knife, a canteen, some matches, and one-third of a silk parachute, with all the nylon strings still attached. The trainees attempted to keep some semblance of order when there were disagreements within the small teams that were put together to try to make it through the mountainous terrain to the various checkpoints.

It being winter, there was little in the way of food to be found in this mostly inhospitable region. No animals were scurrying about for us to try and trap. Although we were told in the pre-survival exercise class that the Cleveland National Forest was home to such animals as mountain lion, bobcat, mule deer, coyote, gray fox, ringtail cat, long-tail weasel, opossum, black-tail jackrabbits, desert cottontails, California ground squirrel, and numerous other small species of rodents, we saw little or no animal life; merely snow and bleak, rocky, mountainous landscape. There also seemed to be nothing fit for human consumption as far as vegetation was concerned, which went along with the fact that during our class there was no mention of any edible plants in this particular wilderness. Water was not a problem, though, as there was snow on the ground, and we were able to start fires in order to melt the snow in our canteens. We were all hungry, very hungry, and eventually ended up eating boiled cactus. We de-thorned the pieces of cactus and boiled the pulpy insides into a semi-palatable soup and mushy vegetable-type solid. We were hoping for tequila, but that did not work out. This tart, unpleasant-tasting mush sustained us for the week in this craggy wasteland. We did see a few deer, and had to keep a watch at night for bobcats and mountain lions that might be drawn by the warmth of our fire. Our only weapons were a knife and a hand-fashioned combination spear and walking stick. Fortunately, the large cats kept their distance. We heard them, but never confronted one.

We had to find and check in at predetermined checkpoints, using the supplied topographical maps. Maps of areas with varying altitudes are very difficult to learn to read. There were some groups that never found the checkpoints and had to be located by search parties in helicopters. Finally, after five days in the forest and mountains, we all ended up at the mock POW camp.

The main gist of SERE training was to provide military personnel with practical experience in the areas of evading capture, survival skills in varying environments, and the Military Code of Conduct. SERE training was established by the U.S. Air Force during the Korean War for the purpose of specially training all those personnel who might be at risk of capture. The training was later expanded to all other branches of the service for the Vietnam conflict.

The Military Code of Conduct is an "ethical" guide, produced by the United States Department of Defense addressing how American military personnel are to act in situations which may contain the possibility of capture by the enemy. It is an important part of military doctrine, but is not considered formal military law in the manner of the Uniform Code of Military Justice or public international law, such as the Geneva Conventions. Included in SERE training was the study of the six articles dealing with the Code of Conduct. These articles (in a somewhat abbreviated version) stated:

    1. I am an American, fighting in the forces that guard and protect my country and I am prepared to give my life in the defense of my country.

    2. I will never surrender of my own free will while I have the means to resist. When I no longer am in a position to inflict injury on the enemy, I have an obligation to evade capture.

    3. If captured, I will continue to resist by all means available, and if the opportunity arises, I will attempt to escape. As a matter of conscious determination a POW must plan to escape, attempt to escape, and assist others attempting to escape. A POW must never seek or accept special favors from his captor.

    4. If I become a prisoner, I will keep faith with my fellow prisoners. I will give no information and take no part in any action that would be detrimental to my fellow captives.

5. When questioned by my captors, I am required only to give my name, rank, service number, and date of birth. (This stipulation is set by the Geneva Conventions.)

6. I will never forget that I am an American, fighting for freedom, responsible for my own actions and dedicated to the principles which made my country free. I will trust in "my" God and the United States.

There was a specific "course" on resisting the enemy in terms of initial capture, followed by instruction on resisting exploitation efforts by the enemy after capture. This harped specifically on the subject of making oral or written confessions and/or apologies. This also included making any recordings, providing any personal histories or creating any material readily usable for propaganda purposes.

We did not have to just walk into the POW camp at the end of the survival exercise. Almost everyone in the class was captured by the roving camp guards as we got closer to the compound. Along with a few other guys, I was not ever captured (I seemed to be quite good at the "evasion" part of the exercise), but eventually, at the sound of a loud siren, we were compelled to turn ourselves in to the guards. It was at that point that the fact that it was merely an "exercise" got a bit foggy. After arriving at the POW camp we were stripped of our clothing, with the exception of our underwear, and sprayed with a water hose. We were then interrogated by the commandant and uniformed soldiers who were Asians playing the role of Vietnamese POW camp-guards. It got hectic, to say the least. We were starved, beaten, interrogated, and kept wet and cold most of the time.

Because of the questionnaires that we had to fill out prior to the training exercise, the guards and interrogators were privy to personal information about each of us. This information was used in the ensuing interrogations. They played on everyone's weaknesses, family relations, and our ethnic make-up. It was not uncommon, during the interrogation process for a guard to use a "prisoner's" wife's, girlfriend's, or mother's name. They also played on the fact that we might be Jewish, or Baptist, or black, or Native American. This "personal" touch in the interrogation sessions gave the "prisoners" a feeling of hopelessness and worry for our loved ones. In a real prisoner situation, we would wonder how they could know all of this information, and what they could possibly do with it. This was all done in order to familiarize us with what would or could happen if we were captured by the enemy. It was all very uncomfortable, scary, and a good incentive to not get caught.

There were a number of participants who ended up signing confessions of war crimes and apologizing for the incursion. It became very "real" in the camp. Men were physically and emotionally abused and hurt,

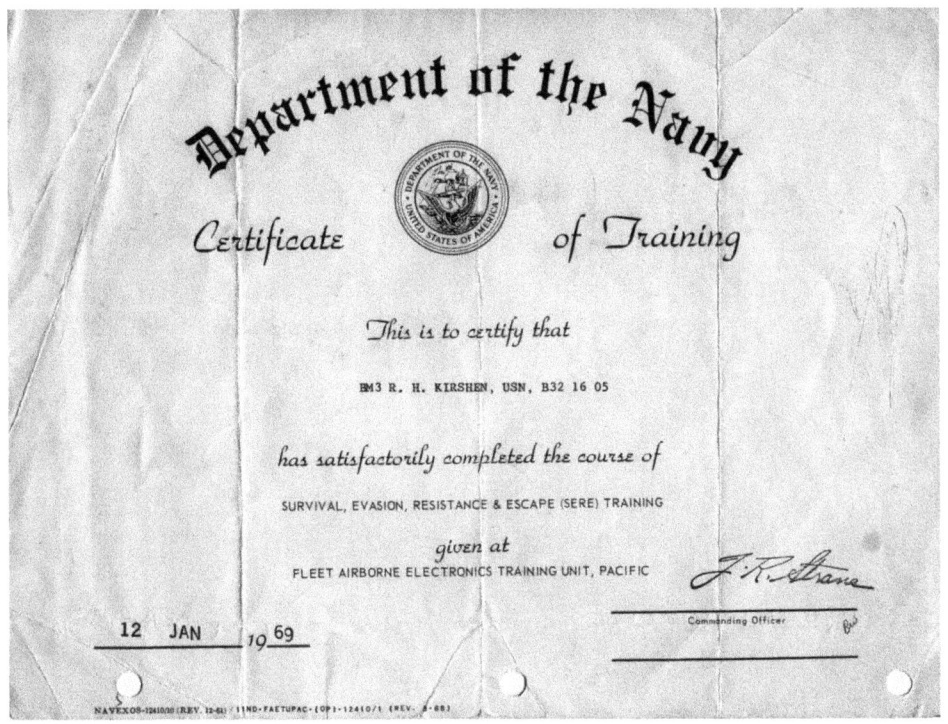

My certificate of completion for the SERE (survival, escape, resistance, evasion) Training Course in Warner Springs, California.

and hopefully only temporarily damaged. I am sure that the constant pangs of hunger, from not eating very much for a week, contributed to the psychological weakness shown by some of the men. This, as well as the constant chill throughout our bodies, made everyone uncomfortable and susceptible. I witnessed men crying, shaking, and being as scared and afraid as they had ever been in their lives. Some just seemed to give up, and retreated into a personal cocoon ... dazed and bewildered, a look of total defeat encumbering their entire being.

That was not a fun place, but I made it through intact, but for a damaged ego, a few bruises, and extreme spasms of hunger. At the end (two days later, which seemed like months) we were all rewarded with the most delicious bologna sandwich in history, given back our clothes, and then returned to the Navy base in San Diego on buses. We smelled horrific, as we had not bathed or showered in over a week, and the barracks, warm showers, and mess hall were a welcome sight to us all. There, we were all given our certificates of completion. Well, not all of us.

```
FLEET AIRBORNE ELECTRONICS TRAINING UNIT, PACIFIC
       U. S. NAVAL AIR STATION, NORTH ISLAND
           SAN DIEGO, CALIFORNIA 92135

                                        06:EWS:FA
                                        3131


RECORD OF SERE TRAINING

THE INDIVIDUAL LISTED ON THE REVERSE SIDE HAS RECEIVED
THE TRAINING LISTED BELOW WHILE ATTENDING THE FAETUPAC
SERE TRAINING SCHOOL COMPLETING ON THE DATE INDICATED

I.   CLASSROOM PHASE

     MORAL ASPECTS AND CODE OF CONDUCT
     SURVIVAL PSYCHOLOGY
     AREA SURVIVAL (TROPIC, DESERT, ARTIC)
     SEA AND SEASHORE SURVIVAL
     EDIBLE FOODS
     LAND TRAVEL
     CAMOUFLAGE AND EVASION
     GENEVA CONVENTIONS
     COMMUNIST INDOCTRINATION METHODS
     POW RESISTANCE AND ESCAPE
     SURVIVAL MEDICINE

II.  FIELD PHASE

     LAND NAVIGATION
     FOOD PROCUREMENT AND PREPARATION
     SHELTER AND FIRE MAKING

III. RESISTANCE LABORATORY PHASE

     CAPTURE
     COMPOUND
     INDOCTRINATION
     INTERROGATION
```

A record of those things covered in the SERE Training Course.

At the debriefing get-together, we also found out that those who had signed confessions, and actually joined the enemy, or apologized to the enemy for the actions of themselves and their country, were going to be reinstituted into the SERE program, and had to repeat it all over again. There were those who thought that failing the course would excuse them

8. Prep-Work for War

from going to Vietnam; the Navy thought otherwise. Loud groans emanated from the audience and those who were destined to repeat were separated from the group and ordered to assemble in another area for a re-orientation of expected behavior. I'm glad I stuck it out. I could now move on to my next duty station: Cam Ranh Bay, Republic of Vietnam.

9

Arrival

After a cursory passport check and an even quicker run through customs, where no one checked our bags, Mary and I were met by a representative of Avalon Cruises. We and another couple were driven to the intercontinental Asiana Hotel. The drive itself was quite an experience: there appear to be no traffic lights or rules in Saigon, and everything seems to move randomly, but everyone gets where they are going. There were literally thousands of Mo-Peds and motor scooters traversing the streets, in what might look to an outsider like total chaos, but in reality was mere bedlam. Maybe to the locals it was also chaotic, and they were just used to it. I kept looking, but could not find the order in anything. Everything between the sidewalks seemed to be in total disarray. Hardly anyone got killed or run over, though, in the half-hour it took to get to the hotel. In some cases, those scooters were sporting 3, 4 or even 5 riders. Two adults, three kids, out for a family outing. It was simply amazing. We even saw a guy with a live pig strapped upside down to his rear seat. I believe that pigs rarely spend time upside down during the course of their lives, so that must have been quite disconcerting for the pig.

We checked in to the hotel and promptly headed to our room, where we both took a much-needed shower, after traveling for almost 30 hours. We saw my cousin Stephen and his wife Debby in the lobby as we checked in. Their flight from Tampa had arrived a couple of hours before ours. Steve informed us that he was signing them both up for a scooter ride through town. I always gave Steve much more credit than that. After all, he is an educated dentist. We declined his offer to join them, as the last half hour was still fresh in our minds, and we would like to live at least a few more days and enjoy the upcoming river cruise. I hoped against hope that Steve and Debbie make it back and would be able to go on the cruise. The British gambling houses set the odds at 6/1 against.

10

How The Hell Had I Ended Up in This Mess Anyway?

World Airways flight #1720, in February of 1969, with ninety others aboard, rolled to a stop on the tarmac in Cam Ranh Bay. Cam Ranh Bay was about one hundred and eighty miles north north-east of Saigon, right on the South China Sea between Phan Rang and Nha Trang. A wheeled stairway was hand-pushed and positioned at the front door. That was before the advent of jet ways. The door opened not only to sweltering heat and oppressive humidity, but also to a U.S. Army master sergeant, who sauntered aboard all spic and span, armed to the teeth, looking open-casket sharp, and announced loudly and somewhat nonchalantly, in a heavy Southern drawl, "Mah name is Sah-gent Woodford, as y'all debahk the plane I want y'all to follah me across the tahrmac in a zig-zag pattuhn, as we ahr undah attack at this time." My eyes widened, my jaw dropped slightly, and I immediately thought to myself, "*Son of a bitch! I've been in this fucking country all of about 90 seconds now, and already someone is shooting at me. I don't think I'm going to like it here. I want to go home ... now!!*"

How the hell had I even ended up here? Oh yeah, now I recall; it's all coming back to me. The short version was that I went out to get the mail one day while lazing about at home. My sister Sandei was with me. I was sure that I would be getting my long-awaited "life changing" check from Publishers Clearing House, but instead, when I went out to check the mail, the only envelope addressed to me was a rather formal notice from my good friends at the Selective Service System. They were informing me that I had been conscripted into the U.S. Army. I decided, on the spot, that it would be much to my advantage to go down and enlist in the Navy immediately rather than take my chances in the army; after all, what would

```
MIAMI              U. S. NAVY RECRUITING SERVICE        HIALEAH
PHONE: 350-5575         101 N.E. 5TH STREET            PHONE: 888-5771
                          MIAMI, FLA.
                              &
                       401 E. 1ST AVENUE
                        HIALEAH, FLA.
                                                   23 January 1967
                                                   _____
                                                        (Date)

To:    Richard H. Kirshen
       _____

Subj:  Application for enlistment in the U. S. Navy; acceptance of

   1.  Your application for enlistment in the United States Navy has been
   accepted by the U. S. Navy Recruiting Service, Report to Navy Proces-
   sing Unit, Armed Forces Examining & Entrance Station, 4100 Aurora,
   Coral Gables, Florida, prior to 7:30 A.M. on  21 Feb 1967    . You
   will depart the same day for the training center and all transportation
   and meals will be furnished.

   2.  Do not bring any of the following articles as they are not permitted
   in the training center: Food, Chewing Gum, Patent Medicine, Drugs,
   Alcoholic Beverages, (Aspirins, BC's etc.), Hotel or Railway Equipment,
   Poker Chips, Playing Cards, Dice, Firearms, Black-Jacks, Brass Knuckles,
   Knives (any size, type, including pen knives), Ammunition, Magazines,
   Books, Electric Shavers, Pictures in glass frames. Do not bring any-
   thing in glass bottles (Hair Tonic, Lotion, Liquid Shoe Polish, etc.) as
   these items may break and spoil your clothing. The Holy Bible is the
   only book that can be taken to the Training Center. Watches, Rings, and
   other valuables should be left at home until after Recruit Training.

   3.  Pay day may be as far away as three weeks, act accordingly as to
   your personal needs, cigarettes, writing material and stamps.

   4.  ~~Suggest that you do not bring in excess of $15.00 with you.~~

   5.  You are to bring five (5) white handkerchiefs and a heavy jacket
   in addition to clothing and toilet articles for five (5) days.

   6.  Please call the ____Miami_____ office in the A.M.
   of the day prior to your departure.

                              Sincerely,


                              _____
                              B. GURLEY, SMC, USN
                              Navy Recruiter
```

The acceptance letter I received from the Navy, accepting my voluntary enlistment into the U.S. Navy.

possibly be my odds of ending up on the ground in Vietnam if I were in the Navy—maybe a million to one? Maybe I would end up somewhere ten or fifteen miles or so out in the South China Sea or the Tonkin Gulf, lobbing eight- or sixteen-inch shells from a cruiser or battleship, toward some unseen target off in the make-believe distance. Under no circumstances

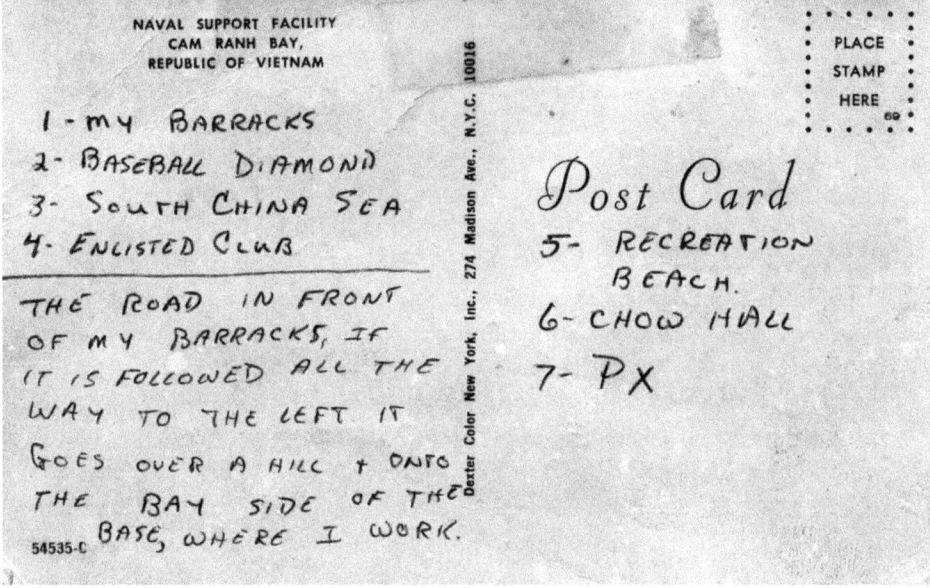

Top and bottom: Front and back sides of a postcard depicting the physical layout of the U.S. Naval Base at Cam Ranh Bay, Vietnam.

would I ever come into contact with the jungle or mountains, or actually have a face-to-face with enemy combatants … or a real war. That just wasn't the way the Navy worked. The Army and Marines did that dangerous stuff, or so I thought. Nevertheless, here I was, boots on the ground, in a war zone, already in grave danger.

The ninety of us reluctantly, and wide eyed, followed the good sergeant across the tarmac in a zigzag pattern and made it safely into what they seriously referred to as a terminal, but more closely resembled a large airplane hangar. I say reluctantly followed the sergeant, because some guys did not want to leave the plane, in hopes, I guess, of somehow staying on board for the return trip … fat chance. On the upside, though (once again, my mother's positive attitude coming to the forefront), I have to admit, there was no long wait at customs or immigration, I didn't have to remove my combat boots and belt, and no one scanned me to see if I had a pen knife, or more than 3 ounces of a liquid or a nail file on me, so we had that going for us.

We breezed on through, and I was picked up by a Navy driver in a jeep and taken across the wide expanse of sand dunes and rolling hills, on a hard-pack road to Naval Support Facility (NSF), Cam Ranh Bay. It was a physically beautiful little piece of land. It looked so serene and undisturbed, lying in the province of Khanh Hoa, between Phan Rang and Nha Trang, right on the shore of the tranquil, azure-blue South China Sea. It had a long wartime history. First, it was used as a staging area for the Russian fleet in 1905 prior to the Battle of Tsushima. After that it became a naval base used by the Japanese just before they invaded Malaysia in 1942. Prior to the U.S. Navy's entering the area in 1964, the French used the bay as a staging area during their ill-fated occupation of Indochina in the 1950s. NSF was a small repair facility guarding the entrance to picturesque Cam Ranh Bay. The views and landscape visible on the jeep ride to the base were most definitely un–Miami like. Exploding mortars and rockets didn't seem to bother the jeep driver as we trekked the 15 kilometers to the Navy base, across the seemingly endless bright green hills and gently rolling sand dunes. I just manned up and pretended it didn't bother me either. But, pathetically, I must admit, as soon as I got to NSF and checked in, I had to go change my underwear. So far, my introduction to Vietnam could be described as unsettling. Miami Beach has little rocket and mortar fire, so I just wasn't properly prepared for this.

11

Touring Saigon

Back at the Hotel Asiana, Steve and Debbie did return from their scooter trip, and after a short walk around the immediate neighborhood, we just hung out in the hotel. There was a meeting scheduled with the tour directors, where they informed all of us as to what to expect and what our upcoming schedule would be. We were then free until the next morning, as some people were still arriving. The four of us grabbed some dinner, joined by another couple on the cruise. We had a few after-dinner drinks, and then crashed early following a very long tiring day.

Upon waking in the hotel the next morning at 7 a.m., Mary and I dressed and headed for breakfast in the dining area off the lobby. The buffet breakfast was sumptuous, offering a multitude of choices. Some of them I had seen before, and some I had never seen on a breakfast buffet, such as spaghetti and meatballs, four different types of soup, fresh opened coconuts with a straw in them, boiled fish, chicken sausage, and different types of noodles.

After breakfast our tour began on a huge bus, and by huge I mean probably the largest vehicle in Vietnam. The bus was the size of a normal tour bus in the U.S., but here, where perspective is skewed by the colossal number of motor scooters, it seemed enormous. The tour was led by Mark Nicholls, our Kiwi (New Zealand) tour guide, and Long, our Vietnamese guide. How this bus traversed the narrow streets of Saigon was quite magical, and we ran over hardly any scooter riders.

We stopped at the Rex Hotel, the five-story, 284-room hotel that, during the Vietnam War, was home to many high ranking military officers and most of the CIA officials who ran the war. Restored now, it was gorgeous, and right in the middle of downtown Saigon. It was now owned by the state, but was first constructed in 1927 by French colonialists. It later underwent renovations, which started in 1959, and its first "guests" arrived

The now unused Presidential Palace in Ho Chi Minh City. Communist leaders have deemed this building a relic of the past to be used exclusively for tourism.

in 1961 in the name of the 57th Transportation Company, from Ft. Lewis, Tacoma, Washington, and the 8th Transportation Company from Ft. Bragg, North Carolina. These were the first company-strength units to arrive in Saigon. Each company arrived with twenty helicopters, and stayed at the Rex for a week, until tents were set up at Tan Son Nhut for the 57th, and up the coast in Quin Nhon for the 8th. The Rex gained its most famous notoriety by hosting the American Military Command's daily conference, which became known by cynical journalists as "The Five O'clock Follies," because it was believed that the optimism shown by the American officers was quite misguided. After a quick excursion through the Rex, we proceeded to the Presidential Palace, and took a tour inside. This is where the official taking over of South Vietnam by North Vietnam took place. It was now known as the Reunification Palace.

Outside the palace, in a place of high honor, under a copse of stately oak trees, was the North Vietnamese Army (NVA) Tank #843. That was the first NVA tank to knock down the gate in front of the palace on April 30, 1975, and gain entry. That exact moment signified the end of the country of South Vietnam, and the unification of the two Vietnams.

The palace proved to be quite fascinating, with all its secretive little rooms. A very informative historical lecture was given by Long during the

11. Touring Saigon

The North Vietnamese tank #843, which was the first tank to enter the Presidential Palace compound and signal the end of the country of South Vietnam.

examination of the three floors of the building. The building was designed by Ngo Viet Thu. The original palace was destroyed in 1962. Construction on the new palace began in July of 1962, and was completed in 1966. While it was being constructed, president Ngo Dihn Diem was assassinated, and government leadership fell into the hands of General Nguyen Van Thieu, who was chairman of the National Leadership Committee, and head of a military junta. Our tour included the opportunity to inspect some of the palace. This included tours of the presidential office and the banquet room, although there are no more presidents, nor any banquets. One can only imagine the chaos, uncertainty, and utter dread that filled the rooms of this building on that fateful last day of the regime, and of the war.

After the Presidential Palace tour, we headed for the War Museum, on the other side of town. The museum commemorated what the Vietnamese referred to as "The American War." This was a distressing and uncomfortable place, because, bear in mind, it was constructed, stocked, and conceived by the North Vietnamese Communists and referred to as the "Agression War Crimes Museum." It was most obviously anti–American, showing countless instances of American-perpetrated horrors and despicable acts thrust upon the Vietnamese people. Some of the stars of this exhibition were napalm, Agent Orange, bombs, bullets, grenades, fighter planes, and helicopters. The main displays consisted of countless photographs of horrors in progress and the resulting

The entryway to the Aggressor War Museum depicting the Communists' side of the "American War," in all of its horror. This is a true propaganda machine, showing the world but one side of the war.

Helicopter and tank display at the Aggressor Museum. Leftover relics of the war, of which America left millions and millions of dollars' worth of equipment and arms.

11. Touring Saigon

damage to property and personnel caused by those weapons and men of war. The effects of utilizing Agent Orange and napalm on the populace, and the land, were shown in graphic detail. Burned and disfigured bodies and charred remains of unidentifiable life forms were numerous. Barren, mile-long fields were depicted in all their dull brown color. Pictures of torture in progress, and mangled, burned, and abused bodies were too abundant to count.

This usually crowded, three-story building was a solemn place, eerily quiet and containing little conversation. Low, unintelligible, murmuring sounds from small groups were heard in the background. The atmosphere was akin to what one would find in places such as the Anne Frank house in Amsterdam, or the Alamo in San Antonio, or Auschwitz in Poland ... solemn, reverent, and a deafening silence throughout.

The museum was filled with people from all corners of the world, walking around bewildered and stunned by what they were witnessing. The images presented to them widened their eyes and dropped their jaws as they openly gaped. They were trying to put some semblance of understanding to what they were observing ... but in most cases, were unable to do so. If you have not experienced war, you cannot truly identify with war and its machinations.

What can one say or think when seeing a beheaded body, or a live person being thrown out of a hovering helicopter a thousand feet above the earth, or the devastating results of napalm coming into contact with a human body? Many of the displays here were left over from the war. Included were tiger cages (small cages lined with barbed wire so that the prisoner inhabitant had very limited movement), a guillotine, and other implements of torture and debasement. Starvation, beatings, withholding water, and hanging by the wrists with the arms behind one's back (this usually ended up with the shoulders being painfully dislocated) were some of the other methods depicted.

As I said, a very distressing and depressing place ... but only showing one side of the brutality. There was, on both sides, enough viciousness and inhumanity to go around. Of course, I felt guilt here; guilt and a slight bit of nausea. After all, I was part of all this. I was here and I participated. I had killed and maimed other human beings for reasons that to this day are still not clear to me, other than to save my own ass. My chest constricted, and breathing became quick and shallow as I took in the sights confronting me and the memories it brought back. Finally, I had to walk out of there, back into the sunshine, where eventually the tightening subsided, my breathing became almost normal once again, and the nausea

"Tiger cages," which were used by the North Vietnamese to keep prisoners in a virtually unmoving, confined position for extended periods of time. Any movement would cause the sharp points from the barbed wire to cut into the unfortunate inhabitant.

dissipated. I let out a huge sigh of relief as I exited. Our tour group, and I imagine every tour group, left there with their own thoughts of those days, and what it must have been like. Every war participant's experiences and perspectives varied widely in a war zone. No one encountered the exact same issues or feelings. It was all dependent on what transpired in your own personal piece of the war, and everyone's piece was different. This visit was the lowlight of my return trip to Vietnam.

After the sobering trip through the War Museum, we headed for a much lighter place as our next point of interest: the Ben Thanh Market. The market place is an indoor market during the day and an outdoor market at night containing booth after booth of vegetables, meat, fish, snails, and crabs. The market was formally established by French Colonial powers in 1859. The original market burned down in 1870, but was rebuilt in 1912, and then renovated in 1985. It was a conglomeration of familiar and some very unfamiliar seafoods, meats, and vegetables. The smells and aromas were overpowering, some good, some almost putrid.

11. Touring Saigon

Evidently, supermarkets are not a big thing here, and the majority of the locals buy everything fresh on the day they intend to use it. We only did the edibles section of the market today, as the other half of the market was inhabited by vendors of all nonedible goods such as clothing, jewelry, accouterments, and what could conceivably be the largest collection of watches in the known world. I never realized until visiting the Saigon Market that Rolex is really spelled "Rolecks." We will get a chance on our own, later, to negotiate that side of the market.

From the marketplace we got back on the bus and headed for the Saigon Culinary Arts Center, which was just the place to help mask the indelible sights of the War Museum, whose shockingly gruesome visual images

A guillotine, which was used mostly upon unfortunate locals, who raised the ire of the Viet Cong or North Vietnamese by collaborating, or seeming to collaborate, with the enemy.

were still fresh in our minds, in spite of the visit to the market. At the Culinary Arts Center we were exposed to a very entertaining hour or so of learning how to marinate chicken, roll a vegetable roll, and watch an expert in the art of Vietnamese cooking perform her magic. She was quite precise with her teaching methods. After watching and listening to her, we all got to attempt to construct our own rolls. Some were perfect (or nearly so), and some not so perfect, as we were assisted and served by a staff of friendly young Vietnamese ladies. As I finished rolling my roll, I jokingly licked the top and rolled it like a joint, and the young Vietnamese lady watching cracked up. She and I had just bonded in a very special way. We had the rolls, beef and noodle soup, marinated chicken and rice, and bananas with some type of tapioca sauce for dessert. This was all accompanied by a bottle (or two) of very cold, very refreshing Saigon beer. All in all, an entertaining experience, before heading back to the bus, and off

Top: The Saigon marketplace. This is the side with fresh vegetables, meats, and seafood, as most Vietnamese shop on a daily basis, only purchasing that which will be used immediately. *Bottom:* One of the numerous fish and seafood stands in the marketplace. Most of the fish shown is sold the same day it is caught.

The Saigon Culinary Arts Center, where both local chefs and interested tourists can take Vietnamese cooking classes ranging from one-day classes to extended classes taking weeks to complete.

11. Touring Saigon

to our hotel for some much-needed rest, or an afternoon of shopping, or whatever we wanted to do.

Mary and I headed for the LaRue corner bar about two blocks from the hotel, where we sat in seats designed for third-graders, out on the sidewalk, and had a nice cold beer. I'm not sure why the seats were so small, even for the diminutive bodies of the Vietnamese. We watched in awe, the constant movement before us. I don't think I had ever seen traffic like I witnessed in Saigon. Thousands of scooters, again, in what outwardly seemed like utter chaos, passed by our corner, barely missing each other, and only fractions of an inch away from a catastrophic multi-vehicle pileup. While sitting there we also noticed the unimaginable tangle of power lines strung across the city. Evidently when a wire breaks, they don't take down and discard the old broken or unusable wires, they just add more, and more, and more wires to the existing poles, which made for a spiderweb of wiring.

Opposite, top: **This is a depiction of the mess that is the electrical system in Saigon. When wires go bad, or break, the old ones are not removed. Another wire is added to the growing mess.** *Opposite, bottom:* **Another example of the constant addition of new wires over old, instead of replacing the bad or broken wires.**

12

My Initial Introduction to Saigon

My first visit into Saigon, back in 1968, was by—guess what—a Navy boat, from Nha Be, about twelve "clicks" (kilometers) down-river from Saigon. Nha Be was the home of the Mobile Riverine Force (MRF). The MRF was a collection of various types of boats designed and matched to riverine warfare. Prior to Vietnam, the Navy had not fought a war on rivers, and was not well suited for the intricacies and demands of such a specialized environment. As luck would have it, wonderfully innovative designers of war craft hopped right on this opportunity, and came up with state-of-the-art war machines designed specifically for the MRF, and this particular war. How fortunate that I was greeted here at Nha Be by all the newly designed and constructed craft. There were four main types of heavily armed river boats.

The Armored Troop Carrier, or Tango Boat (ATC), was 56.5 feet long, weighed sixty-six tons, had a crew of seven, and could do 8.5 knots. It was armed with four M-1919 Browning 50-caliber machine guns, two MK-16 20MM cannons, one MK-19 grenade launcher, one 81MM mortar, and a 105MM howitzer cannon.

The Monitor Boat was sixty-one feet long, carried a crew of eleven, and could do 8.5 knots. It was armed with one 81MM mortar, one 40MM cannon, one 20MM cannon, two Mark 18 grenade launchers, three M-79 grenade launchers, two 50-caliber machine guns, and four M-60 machine guns. It could also be converted to carry either a 105MM Howitzer cannon, or a 200MM flamethrower. It was, basically, a floating tank. Its name came from its slight resemblance to the famous American Civil War ironclad of the same name.

The Assault Support Patrol Boat, or Alpha Boat (ASPB), was fifty

12. My Initial Introduction to Saigon

One of the heavily armed Monitor river boats, carrying the largest weaponry of any of the boats that patrolled the rivers.

feet long, weighed 36.5 tons, was made of quarter-inch steel, had a five-man crew, and could do nine knots. It was armed with two Mark-48 turrets containing either twin 20MM cannons or twin 50-caliber machine guns, two M-60 machine guns, one 81MM mortar, and a dragging chain for finding river mines.

Another boat on the rivers was the lighter, faster Patrol Boat River (PBR), a thirty-two-foot, Jacuzzi water jet–powered fiberglass boat, capable of over thirty knots. It carried a four-man crew and was powered by twin V6-53 GM diesel engines. Its armament consisted of twin 50-caliber machine guns (in a forward-mounted 180-degree turret), twin M-60 machine guns, one 40MM MK-19 grenade launcher, and one more 50-caliber machine gun, mounted aft. This is the boat featured in *Apocalypse Now* and is the boat that most people think about when referring to the river war in Vietnam.

In addition to those heavily armed boats, there were the troop and supply transport boats. Those were the Landing Craft, Mechanized (LCM's). They came in two sizes: the LCM-8, which was seventy-nine feet long, weighing sixty-nine tons; and the LCM-6, which was forty-nine feet long and weighed forty tons. These boats could carry whatever weapons

One of the Tango boats, the most heavily armored river boat, with armor plating surrounding the entire boat.

the captain decided on. Usually there were two 50-caliber machine guns mounted on the stern, two M-60 machine guns, unmounted, and fired from the well-deck, one grenade launcher, and each crew member's personal M-16.

I designed, and had made in a local tailor shop, my first boat's emblem and patch. I ended up on many different boats over the course of my nine months on the rivers. The alteration shops in town could copy anything, and could embroider whatever anyone desired or designed. I merely showed them a picture of what I wanted, and voila, they produced it perfectly. My boat crew wore the patches on those occasions that we actually wore shirts.

Nha Be is where I first became a boat captain, after arriving at the MRF headquarters and being asked by a lieutenant, "Ever drive a boat, son?" Lightheartedly, I replied with outstretched arms and a twinkle in my eyes, "Hey, I'm from Miami!" with the implication that I was wholeheartedly joking. Unfortunately, he failed to see the humorous intent, and quickly and seriously responded, "Good, a qualified boat captain. Here's your boat." He pointed to an LCM-8 boat, armed with port and starboard–mounted 50-caliber machine guns, two unmounted M-60s, one single-

12. My Initial Introduction to Saigon

shot unmounted M-79 grenade launcher, the crew's personal M-16s, and one weapon I had never seen before: the Honeywell belt-fed, hand-cranked grenade launcher. It fired 40MM grenades, just like the M-79, a maximum of 300 yards, as fast as you could crank the handle. Awesome!

The LCM was powered by four GM 6-71 diesel engines and could attain a top speed in the neighborhood of 14 to 18 knots, when empty. She wasn't pretty and she wasn't fast, but she was made of steel, not fiberglass. I saw that as an important positive attribute in a place where metal bullets constantly obliterated fiberglass boats and their inhabitants. I would take "slow and steel" over "fast and glass" every time, bearing in mind that neither one can outrun a bullet ... but a bullet won't shatter steel.

My personally designed patch for the LCM-8 boat, which was the first boat where I was designated captain. We ferried arms, troops and supplies up and down various rivers.

I was stunned at the lieutenant's response, and tried to explain that I was kidding, but he had already handed me a requisition sheet to fill out for my first trip up river, which would be preceded by a trip into Saigon to pick up some supplies for the base.

I chose a crew, and after looking at the manual and learning how to start the four diesel engines, I checked all my gauges and headed to Saigon, having no idea how to get there. Fortunately for us, there was another boat going, and I followed him.

My crew was made up of John from Chicago, Dale from Wisconsin, and Dennis from Kansas. I didn't have any way of scientifically picking a crew from the multitude of guys who were awaiting assignment and available, so I narrowed it down to one very important, probing question: "You smoke grass?" If I got a positive response, I picked him for my crew. After all, I am from Miami, and I firmly believed in the centuries-old adage, dating back to Columbus, and maybe even as far back as the Phoenicians, "A Mellow Crew is a Happy Crew." Seriously, that is not a centuries-old adage; I made it up, but it all worked out fine.

Now, if you will, please make note that neither Chicago, Wisconsin,

Three of my crew members getting mentally ready to take a trip up-river. We all needed something to deal with the uncertainty, and the distinct possibility of not returning.

nor Kansas is anywhere near an ocean. I repeatedly crossed paths with guys like this in the Navy, and always wondered about it: guys who had never seen an ocean in their entire lives joined the Navy. That just astounded me. Furthermore, most of them, since they were from middle America, and went to boot camp at Great Lakes Naval Recruit Training Center near Chicago, never did get to see an ocean until they arrived at their first duty stations after boot camp. What if they found out that they hated the ocean? What if they suffered from thalassophobia (a fear of the ocean)? What if they had a salt allergy?

We arrived at the supply dock on the teeming Saigon River and I pulled into a spot just about 2 feet bigger than my boat, between two huge ships that were tied up at the wharf. As I got off my boat, it just so happened

12. My Initial Introduction to Saigon

that an admiral was walking down the pier with his entourage. Admirals never seem go anywhere alone. They are like the Navy's rock stars. He stopped and said, "Nice parking job, sailor!" I saluted, and in my best "weathered sailor" voice retorted, "Thank you, sir, I can drive the crate this piece of garbage came in."

At this point I inwardly thanked my grandfather and my uncle for teaching me about seamanship and boat handling. For many years, I joined them fishing in Miami and up north in their summer home, on the south shore outside of Boston. Boats and the ocean had always been a big part of my family and my life. Also, prior to coming down here to the Delta, I had been stationed up the coast a bit, in Cam Ranh Bay, and my job there required me to drive a smaller LCM-6 boat. Because of all this, I had a pretty good idea as to how to handle the boat. The admiral raised an eyebrow at my response, then just chuckled at my retort, and continued down the pier to do whatever it was that admirals did.

Fortunately, we left one crewman on the boat as the rest of us meandered off in search of the person who was supposed to know why we were there. I say "fortunately," because the tide differential in the Saigon River is about 7 to 8' between low and high tide, which, of course, I was never informed of. This made it quite advantageous, as well as necessary, to leave someone on a tied-up boat in order to loosen and tighten the mooring lines in accordance with the changing depths of the river water. This was another one of the Navy's "on the Job training" exercises. How do you forget to tell someone that? Why was I not informed? Anyway, we eventually got what we came for and headed back to Nha Be, where we unloaded the base supplies, and then loaded our own provisions and ammo for our first trip up river.

13

Eating

Mary and I returned to the hotel and relaxed for a while before meeting downstairs again for our nighttime foray to the Avalon Cruise–sponsored get-together dinner. Hoi An, a beautifully appointed restaurant, about a fifteen-minute ride from the hotel in the old section of town, had a section reserved just for our party of thirty-plus. Our dinner came in courses, including spring rolls, papaya salad with shrimp and pork, sautéed chicken with lemon grass and chili, Vietnamese spinach with garlic, steamed rice in coconut milk, and ice cream. With the Vietnamese, presentation seems to be as important as the actual taste of the food. Everything was served on beautiful dinnerware, and each plate was adorned with decorative and colorful garnish.

Dinner was accompanied by an entertaining and talented three-piece musical group who played throughout our meal. The trio consisted of one man on a lute-type instrument and a woman with something equivalent to a lap steel guitar, with arced strings, plucked by smooth wooden picks attached to each of her fingers. The third member of the trio was an extraordinarily beautiful woman playing what I later learned was an instrument called a du xian qin (doo-shan-keen, or, lone string zither). The instrument had a hollow rectangular, intricately appointed wood body with but one silk string, close to three feet long. The string was attached fast at one end, and about four inches up on a curved, ebony wood stick at the other end, which was perpendicular to the base and slightly moveable. This allowed the musician to change the tension on the string, producing a host of sounds, seemingly impossible from an instrument with but one string. The workmanship was extraordinary. This was a delightfully entertaining performance by this talented trio. After another fine dinner, we boarded the bus and headed back to the hotel, hitting even fewer scooter riders this time. Mary and I, and Steve and Debbie hung out

13. Eating

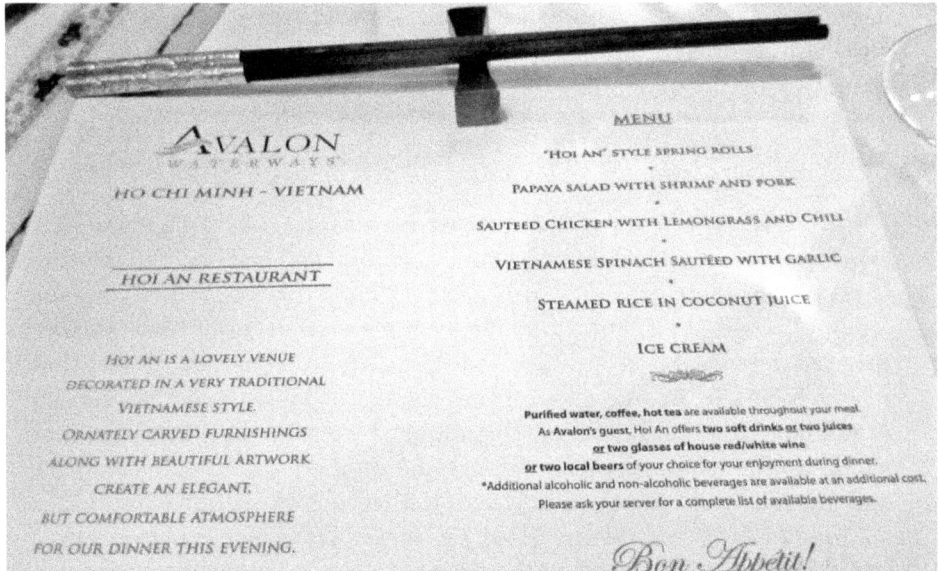

The Hoi An Restaurant in downtown Saigon. Menu specifically drawn up for the Avalon Cruise guests.

at the lobby library/bar, and after a few jokes and a few drinks we retired for the evening.

Certainly those meals that we had been enjoying so far had no resemblance whatsoever to the meals I ate on my first trip to Vietnam, so many years ago. I cannot recollect even one meal during the war that was accompanied by a musical group. The meals at the bases where I was stationed, such as Nha Be and Cam Ranh Bay, could not be classified as terrible by any means, and even consisted of the occasional steak dinner and maybe a lobster or two upon occasion. It was the meals we were forced to endure while on patrol on the river boats, and at the Advanced Tactical Support Bases (ATSBs) intermittently spaced along the rivers, that vaulted across the gap that separated average from awful. C-rations were not personally satisfying for long-term subsistence, in spite of what the military authorities tried to convince us of. (Each meal came with its own military approved can opener.) In actuality, C-rats weren't even good for short-term subsistence. Some were absolutely vile, while others were merely unpalatable.

The ATSBs served food that ranked one level above C-rations, but still two levels below tasty. Their offerings improved from laughably awful to disappointingly bad. But at least the food on the ATSBs was hot, more often than not, and was not left over from World War II. The ATSBs had a makeshift kitchen on at least one of the floating barges that made up those bases. They generally served sandwiches, soups, and mystery meals. The cooks were given a vast amount of leeway with their culinary innovations, depending on exactly what supplies they received at any given time.

My first experience with C-rations, on my boat, was not a wonderful experience at all, although it was quite memorable. I had decided that the C-ration spaghetti (the "C" in C-ration stands for "canned," or maybe "crappy") would be significantly tastier if it were hot, or at least warmer than tepid. Since it is very difficult to start a fire on a boat, not to mention relatively unsafe, I came up with the idea that if I just heated up the can of military pasta on the engine manifold as we rode the river, then that would do the job quite nicely. Well, it did do the job most satisfactorily, and not only that, it turned into yet another one of my more important learning or "aha!" moments. What I garnered from that experience was that if you put a small hole in the top of the can prior to putting the can on the engine to warm up, the can will not explode and cover your engine room with spaghetti. Tsk tsk, once again, you live and you learn.

14

CU CHI, MR. NAM AND THE TUNNELS

Following a night of intermittent sleep, Mary and I got out of bed at 6 a.m. and headed for the wonderful buffet breakfast again, trying new things. Pad thai, pho, dumplings, baguette, and the ever-popular fresh coconut were some of the local delights. After breakfast, we headed for Cu Chi, aboard the bus, and for the first hour, our guide, Mark, did a wonderfully enlightening dissertation on the somewhat recent history of Vietnam, and the once again rising tensions in Southeast Asia, Australia, and countries in the surrounding area. These tensions were being fueled by China's insistence on gaining a foothold on the huge oil reserves in the Tiananmen Sea. They are angering not only Vietnam and the Philippines, but also Australia and other Pacific nations by their incursions into some of the outlying islands that previously were not being disputed. Who knows where this will eventually lead?

On the way to Cu Chi we made one stop, at a rubber tree plantation that was still in operation and still producing rubber. The ride to Cu Chi took about an hour and forty-five minutes, and as we pulled into the parking lot of the home of the famous Viet Cong tunnel systems, we saw that this was, indeed, a very popular spot to visit, not only by tourists, but by locals alike. Every parking spot was occupied, and people were milling around everywhere. Cu Chi was home to one of the most intricate tunnel systems used by the Viet Cong (VC) during the war, with hundreds of entrances hidden in the jungles. The tunnels went for over thirty kilometers, sometimes at three levels, all the way to Saigon. People lived in seemingly unlivable conditions.

We sat through a lecture by our guide, Long, who then introduced Mr. Nam, an ex–Viet Cong soldier who had spent a considerable amount

A stop along the way to the Cu Chi tunnels at a rubber tree plantation. The plantation is still a working business. The guide showed us the oozing rubber from the trees.

of time in the Cu Chi tunnels during the war. During one attack he lost his right arm and the sight in his left eye. He explained how some of his comrades lived in the tunnels, off and on, for months at a time, subsisting on rice cakes, and whatever they could forage when they went out at night. Underground wells, hospitals, cooking, and living conditions inside the tunnels were explained.

While he was reminiscing, I recalled thinking, when I was driving a patrol boat nearby: *Where do these people live? What do they do? How can they ambush us and then disappear?* I just didn't get it. I was well aware that we had a huge U.S. Army occupation near this location on the rivers, but how could the Viet Cong keep avoiding them? I had absolutely no idea as to the intricacy of the VC tunnel system, or that it even existed. It just never crossed my mind that people could and would live underground for extended periods of time, pop up intermittently to wreak havoc, and then disappear once again. I don't believe that I could personally ever be so dedicated to any cause strong enough to agree to live underground.

14. Cu Chi, Mr. Nam and the Tunnels   71

Riding on the rivers back then presented many questions like these to those of us who participated in that part of the war. The rivers meandered and turned frequently, often in right angles, sometimes in doglegs, sometimes in oxbows (an approximate 270-degree turn). Straightaways were infrequent, and when they did appear, they did not last long. From a bird's-eye view it just looked like so many giant brown snakes slithering through the jungle .The few times that I flew over the Mekong Delta area, I was amazed at the number of rivers and tributaries that crossed this region.

Mr. Nam was humble, but proud, in his presentation as to what it was like to be a Viet Cong soldier. He was asked questions by the rest of our contingent, and he answered them all. Our guide, Mr. Long, expertly interpreted for him. Mr. Nam even imparted to us about how he had lost his arm in an artillery explosion, and what type of medical treatment he had received. He was asked what he did for the cause after his "accident," and proudly answered that he did clerical and support work, but he never

Mr. Nam, a former Viet Cong soldier, gave an interesting and introspective talk, aided by our guide. He lost an arm and an eye in the war.

lost his drive or determination to defeat the infiltrators. He was asked if claustrophobia was ever a problem with the men in the tunnels. He conveyed to us that those men were so focused on their objective that claustrophobia was never a problem. Later, after some independent research, I learned that many thousands of the VC tunnel soldiers had suffered irreparable mental and physical damage due to their particularly demanding duty.

I learned that life in the tunnels was far more difficult and challenging for the men who had to endure it than Mr. Nam had let on in his talk. Air, water and food were scarce and the tunnels were inhabited by not only the VC, but also by ants, poisonous centipedes, spiders, and innumerable rats and other vermin. For much of the time, the soldiers spent their days in the tunnels working or resting, coming out only at night to scavenge for food and supplies, tend to crops, and engage the enemy in battle. Many times, during heavy enemy operations or during bombing runs, they were forced to remain underground for many days at a time. Sickness was widespread among the tunnel dwellers, especially malaria, which was listed as the second most common cause of death, next to enemy encounters, among the VC who lived there. One captured VC document stated that at any given time close to half of any VC unit had malaria, and almost one hundred percent had intestinal parasites. American soldiers coined the term "Black Echo" to describe the conditions within the tunnels.

After the lecture I introduced myself to Mr. Nam, through the interpreter, and explained to him that I was nearby, patrolling the Vam Co Dong on my boat, while he was here. He told me that "those damned boats" were a bane to his very existence. He often thought what a terrible job that must be, being shot at from clandestine spots along the river, living unprotected from the elements, and having to be in a constant state of total mental awareness. Unbelievably to me, here's a guy who was subjected to living underground in a tunnel, and he thought that I had a dreadful job. I guess everything really does boil down to perspective. We shook left hands, and our eyes met momentarily. There was no animosity, no hate, and no anger. I believe there was but a mutual understanding of what we had endured separately but simultaneously during those ominous and dangerous days, and that now it was over and but a mere blurring memory—albeit a memory never to be forgotten.

After my discussion with Mr. Nam, we continued on with our examination of the Cu Chi tunnel area, actually going through one of the tunnels, observing how the air vents were constructed and so well hidden. The VC were ingenious. They had figured out how to live and hide under-

14. Cu Chi, Mr. Nam and the Tunnels

One of our tour group heading up out of one of the tunnels. The only thing changed by the tourist authorities was the entryway to the tunnels. All else remained as it was during the war.

ground for extended periods of time. For ventilation purposes they had pounded long pieces of bamboo from the surface down into the tunnels, usually at the base of a tree, so that it was less noticeable. After the bamboo poles were pounded into the ground, and in a matter of weeks, termites would eat away the bamboo (yes termites eat bamboo), leaving just the holes. There were thousands of these ventilation holes, without which it would not have been possible to live in the tunnels.

We were then shown an assortment of booby traps, and were told how they were used mainly as psychological warfare by the Viet Cong against the invading enemy. They did not usually kill the poor unsuspecting victim, but instead crippled him or inflicted massive infections requiring amputations. They were frightful and devious in their design. They were also diversionary, as they caused the enemy troops to constantly check the ground for traps. The booby traps were typically made up of sharpened bamboo or metal spikes, sticking up vertically from the bottom of holes in the ground camouflaged with foliage, grass, or dirt. They were

14. Cu Chi, Mr. Nam and the Tunnels

constructed in an array of designs, and the spikes were often spread with animal or human feces, which was the cause of the infections in the resulting wounds. According to U.S. Army statistics, 11 percent of all deaths and 17 percent of all wounds to Americans were attributed to the booby traps.

We next saw how the rice cakes were made, which was a main staple in the tunnels. Without these rice cakes, the tunnel people would have starved, or been unable to subsist underground for the amount of time they did.

There were also displays of the many different types of weapons used by both sides. Shown in the glass cases were Kalashnikov AK-47 machine guns, M-16s, M-60 medium-weight machine guns, M-79 single-shot grenade launchers, and B-40 rockets and their launchers. I had never seen most of the weapons used by the Viet Cong, but had seen the effects of many of them, as my boat, my crew, and I were frequently targeted by these weapons.

After this very enlightening and informative tour, we boarded our bus and headed back toward Saigon. On the way, we stopped at the Indochine Restaurant for lunch and were treated to a very appetizing meal of vegetable soup, pomelo salad (a large pear-shaped citrus fruit, with very thick rind, weighing from 2 to 4 lbs., native to Southeast Asia), stir-fried morning glory (a semi-aquatic tropical plant grown as a vegetable, fried rice with pork and shrimp, grilled chicken, beef filet rolled with pear, and ice cream with fried banana. It was another of the great meals we encountered in Saigon.

After lunch, we headed back to the hotel, where Mary and I, and Steve and Debbie, went up to our rooms to wash up and change our sweaty clothes. We met back in the lobby at 3:30, clean and refreshed, and walked into downtown Saigon again. The walk took twenty minutes as we passed many storefronts selling everything from CDs, to jewelry, to silk clothing. We wanted to run over to the marketplace to do some shopping, as this would be our last chance to do so before boarding the boat tomorrow. We did our shopping as the day grew later, which meant the traffic was slowly increasing from unbearable to total insanity. We stopped at the rooftop

Opposite, top: The hole at the bottom of the tree was used to get air down to the tunnels. There were thousands of these holes, without which living in the tunnels would have been impossible. *Opposite, bottom:* One of the many types of booby traps our troops had to deal with in the jungles. Most did not cause death, but inflicted debilitating physical and mental wounds on the unfortunate victims.

14. Cu Chi, Mr. Nam and the Tunnels

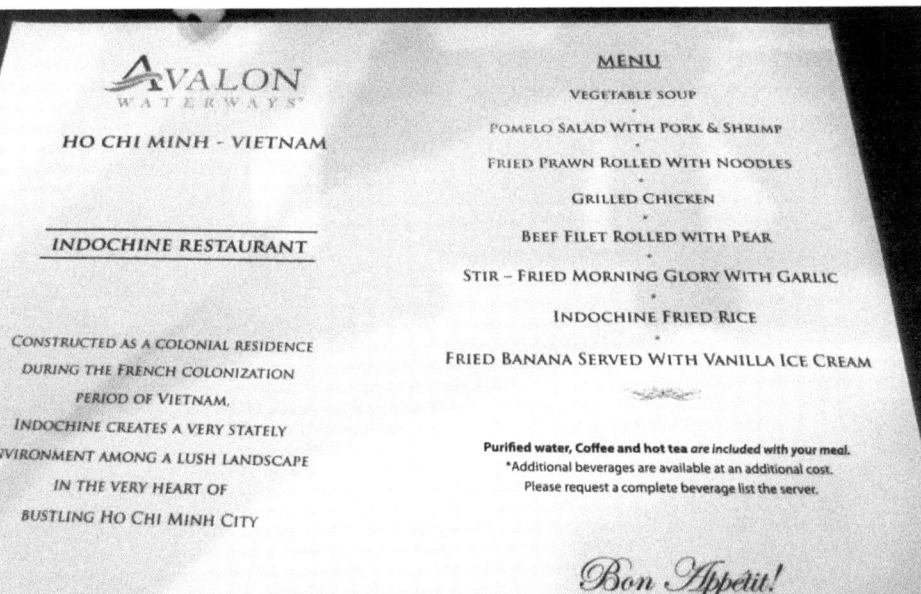

The menu from our lunch at the Indochine. Both the menu and the lunch were specific to the Avalon Tour group.

bar at the Rex Hotel for a nice cold beer. Our table was right along the edge of the roof and afforded us a view of the street below. We watched the thousands of scooters on the wide boulevard act out what looked like an electronic game from where we sat. Unbelievably, to them, there still seems to be some kind of order, but I only see the bedlam that is an everyday occurrence here.

While sipping a cold one at the plush rooftop bar at the Rex, we noticed that our waiter had a mole under his chin, with the longest mole hair in the history of the world. It could be tucked into his shirt pocket if he wanted to, or possibly spun into a nice area rug. I wondered if the Guinness Book of World Records had a category for mole hair length.

We took a slow, careful walk back to the hotel, attempting to avoid

Opposite, top: A woman at the Cu Chi tunnel exhibit showing how to make rice cakes. These rice cakes were the main food staple of the Viet Cong, and could be made underground in the tunnels. *Opposite, bottom:* Our tour group having lunch at the Indochine Restaurant, on our way back to Saigon from Cu Chi. Once again, the food and the presentation were fantastic.

being swept into the unending torrent of vehicles. It's almost like playing a live version of the old "Frogger" game. Back at our hotel, oasis from the bedlam, we were tired, decided to skip dinner, and retired to our rooms for a much-needed rest.

15

Operation Giant Slingshot

I had been to Cu Chi previously. Well, not exactly into the city, but as one side of the city is bordered by the Saigon River, the south side is bordered by the Vam Co Dong. The Vam Co Dong is a river I patrolled while attached to the Mobile Riverine Force, out of Nha Be. It went past Cu Chi, past Tay Ninh City, and straight across the border into Cambodia. The Vam Co Tay and the Vam Co Dong converged at what was named the "Parrot's Beak," a part of Cambodia that jutted into Vietnam.

Our mission was dubbed Operation Giant Slingshot, as that is the shape that the course of the two rivers took when they "split up" around the Parrot's Beak. That was a hotly contested area of the country then, inhabited by the U.S. Army's 25th Infantry Division, as the Ho Chi Minh Trail (the main supply route for the enemy) had its terminus just west, at the Vietnam/Cambodia border. My mission, and the mission of Operation Giant Slingshot, was to help stop the flow of arms and supplies to the Viet Cong and North Vietnamese Army that came all the way from the north, down the Ho Chi Minh Trail, destined to resupply the troops in the south. Our other objective was to protect the Long Tau shipping channel into Saigon, which was an instrumental lifeline for the city.

We stopped and inspected every boat we came across on the rivers. The majority of the time we found nothing, but often we came across and confiscated weapons, ammo, food, and supplies. We commandeered these boats, towed them and their now securely bound crews (we were Navy, and we knew knots) to the closest friendly base, and turned them over.

They rarely resisted us, but on occasion we were pressed to use force to capture and secure the boats and crews. These instances sometimes turned messy and deadly. Occasionally, we watched and protected other

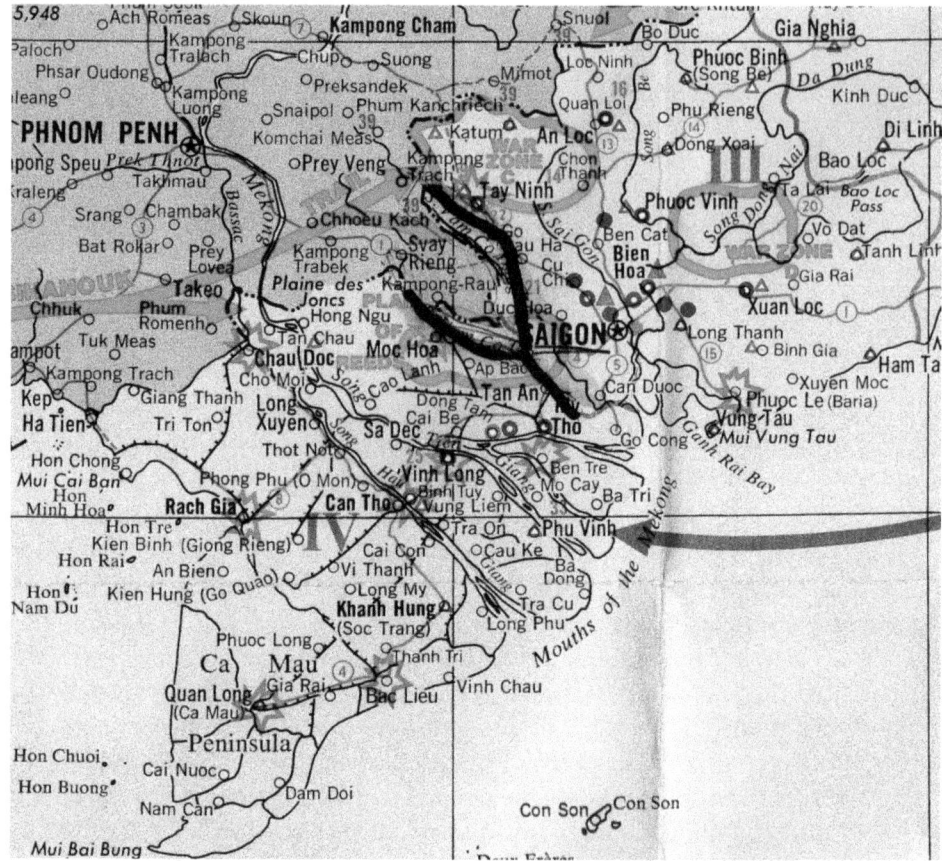

Map of the Saigon and Delta area, with black lines highlighting Operation Giant Slingshot.

patrol boats as they interdicted indigenous boats to search for contraband.

Fierce fighting and very heavy bombing was the norm for this entire area of the country. Both sides took heavy losses. This is where one of the boats I captained was hit with a B-40 rocket, and sunk. The rocket actually went entirely through one of our V6-53 diesel engines. It went right through the entire engine block of the outboard port engine and part of the way through the starboard engine. The boat sank in a matter of minutes, and my crew and I were eventually picked up by one of the other boats in our group. (This experience will be related in more detail in a later chapter.) The excitement never stopped. I was taken back to Nha Be, reunited with the rest of my crew, and issued another boat almost imme-

15. Operation Giant Slingshot

Our .50-caliber machine gun armed and ready as we pass a small village and local sampan on our way up-river. You never knew who was who in Vietnam.

diately after my concussion had subsided. It was sort of like, "Oh, you lost a boat? Here, we have another one. You leave tomorrow."

This time, the brains behind this whole operation allowed an entirely new vision of Operation Giant Slingshot to travel to the forefront of their inane ideas. We were to take Navy Seabees (CBs-Construction Battalions) up to the Cambodian border in my newly gifted LCM-8. We carried both men and bulldozers in our boat. The idea was to start at the border and clear the jungle back fifty yards on each side of the river, so that the enemy could not set up jungle-borne ambushes any more. Well, on paper, that sounded like a great idea. Not really. In reality it could never work, as the slow and tedious job of knocking down the jungle with bulldozers was hindered greatly by the fact that it grew back behind us as we moved along, in only a matter of weeks.

When we first got to the border, I pulled the boat up to the shore of the river and let down the ramp so that the bulldozers could roll out. I

CERTIFICATE OF APPOINTMENT

To all who shall see these presents, greeting:

Know Ye, that by authority vested in me and reposing special trust and confidence in the patriotism, valor, fidelity and abilities of

RICHARD HOWARD KIRSHEN

I do hereby appoint you to the rate of

BOATSWAIN'S MATE SECOND CLASS

in the

UNITED STATES NAVY

to rank as such from the 16TH day of OCTOBER, nineteen hundred and 69

TO THE APPOINTEE

Your appointment carries with it the obligation that you exercise increased authority and willingly accept greater responsibility. Occupying now a position of greater authority, you must strive with a renewed dedication toward the valued ideal of service with honor.

You are charged with demonstrating a proper example of performance, moral courage, and dedication to the Navy and the Nation. Your every action must be governed by a strong sense of personal moral responsibility in order that, by example and leadership, subordinates will contribute their utmost to the effectiveness and efficiency of the United States Navy.

Given under my hand at U. S. NAVAL SUPPORT FACILITY, CAM RANH BAY, VIETNAM this 16TH day of OCTOBER in the year of our Lord nineteen hundred and 69

W. E. JANES, COMMANDER, U. S. NAVY
COMMANDING OFFICER
U. S. NAVAL SUPPORT FACILITY
CAM RANH BAY, VIETNAM

NAVPERS 1430/8 (USN) (5-67)
S/N-0105-902-2380

My certificate of appointment to the rank of E-5, or Petty Officer 2nd Class (equivalent to a sergeant in the Army).

was in the pilothouse, at the stern of the boat, as usual, manning the controls, keeping the bow fast to the landing area along the river bank. I lowered the six-ton mechanized ramp at the bow, the bulldozer started, and a few men rushed off the front of the boat to stand guard duty. I watched them, uninterestedly, from my raised vantage point on the stern.

15. Operation Giant Slingshot

The second man off the boat stepped about 10 feet into the jungle and hit a tripwire. A small explosion went off and I watched, disbelieving, as the man's head disappeared from his body and a column of blood spurted straight up into the air. This was a sight my brain didn't register immediately. My eyes widened, my jaw slacked, my head tilted to the right, and I watched in awe as his body stayed erect and motionless for a few seconds, then crumpled slowly to the earth, like a blow-up doll with a leak. He had hit a concealed chest-high tripwire attached to a grenade booby trap that was set into the split end of a bamboo pole sticking up about 5 feet from the ground. Pandemonium erupted. After all, these were Navy Seabees, not real soldiers. They were used to building and repairing things, not recovering headless bodies. Back home, most of them would have been redneck hard-hat construction workers. I got sick to my stomach and turned and vomited. I tried vainly to remove that image from my brain. It's still there. The bulldozers were eventually offloaded and the Seabees began their arduous and futile task of attempting to remove the jungle. The boat crew and I just moved along the river with them.

My second class petty officer designation patch, worn on the left sleeve of my dress blues, with the crossed anchors showing my rate as boatswain's mate (bosun's mate).

After this incident, and a few others in which my crew and I were involved in firefights, the Navy awarded us with advancement in rank. In the Navy, in order to advance in rank, one had to take a written test, and depending on how many of each rank the Navy needed at any given time, the men with the highest scores were advanced. In a war zone, that test could be eliminated and one could receive a field promotion to the next rank if recommended by his superior officers, and if one's actions deemed that honor. I was given a field promotion to petty officer second class (E-5) because of numerous actions on the rivers. I made second class petty officer (equivalent to a sergeant in the Army) two years and seven months after entering boot camp. I was told at the time that that was the quickest rise by anyone to E-5 in the Navy since the end of World War II.

16

THE POST OFFICE AND THE *ANGKOR*

Up early again, and down to breakfast around 6 a.m., Mary and I decided (actually Mary decided) that we needed to do a bit more shopping. So it was off to the Main Saigon Post Office. Rarely had we ever decided to go shopping and ended up in a post office. But this was, by far, no ordinary

The Saigon Post Office, designed early in the century by Gustav Eiffel, of Eiffel Tower fame. There are many examples of his work in Southeast Asia.

The *Avalon Angkor*, our home for eight days on the river. It was large enough (sixteen staterooms) to be comfortable, and small enough to be able to tie up anywhere along the river for side trips.

The walkway along the port side of the *Avalon Angkor*, showing entrances to the first-floor staterooms. All rooms had full river views.

post office. It has a neoclassical architectural style and was designed and constructed by Gustav Eiffel, of Eiffel Tower fame. It was built in the late 19th century (1886–1891), when Vietnam was French Indochina. The two north and south walls are covered by mural-maps of Vietnam as it was in 1892. Secondly, it had not one, but two gift shops. We strolled leisurely through both gift shops, bought a few souvenirs, and then headed back to the hotel to pack.

While my wife was shopping, I took the opportunity to snap a few interior shots of some of the local women, in the mahogany and tile–decorated post

16. The Post Office and the Angkor

The Phu My Bridge over the Saigon River. All boats and ships leaving Saigon for the South China Sea or the Mekong River must go under this bridge.

office lobby. The women were still as beautiful as I remembered from my last trip, only now a bit more Westernized.

After packing, we left our suitcases outside the hotel room to be picked up by Avalon, and then headed down to the lobby. We then boarded the bus for the ride to the boat, and our upcoming river cruise. After a fifteen-minute jaunt through Saigon, we arrived at the Saigon River and our new home for the next seven days, the *Avalon Angkor*. It was beyond my expectations.

The *Avalon Angkor* was gorgeous, like something out of a Humphrey Bogart movie, appointed in beautiful teakwood, mahogany, and brass. Everything was spit shined and neat. It was, simply put, immaculate.

After boarding, we received our safety lecture. We then checked out our room, which was elegant, but not overstated. All of the rooms had views of the river from the beds.

We soon untied, departed the wharf, and headed slowly down the Saigon River. As hundreds of boats traversed the river, all the passengers mingled along the handrails and watched as the now modern city of Saigon passed by.

17

Nha Be

An hour after leaving Saigon, we passed Nha Be, the Mobile Riverine base twelve miles south of Saigon where I was stationed during part of the war. The original objective of the base was to patrol and protect the water approaches to Saigon, escort military and commercial vessels, and keep the shipping channels free of enemy mines. It later became home to the Navy's River Patrol Force, operating against Viet Cong waterborne traffic in the Mekong Delta and the Rung Sat Special Zone.

I shuddered slightly as I recalled that place and my time spent there. Nha Be, the "Jewel of the Delta" (I just made that up), home of the Mobile Riverine Force (MRF), where I was the captain of numerous river patrol boats, was now a tank farm, with huge storage tanks for fuel, or cooking oil, or something. Maybe those tanks were full of nuc mam, the fish sauce that the Vietnamese used on everything. It is the Vietnamese soy sauce.

Nha Be is no longer the teeming war-boat refuge it once was with the hustle and bustle of hundreds of boats coming in and out of its dockage area, boats with the telltale signs of riverine warfare strafed across their shattered and damaged hulls. Dirty, unshaven, battle-weary sailors returning for a few days rest before going back out. Now, it just sits there, at the juncture of the Long Tau and the Soi Rap Rivers, serving a much more mundane purpose than it once did. It looked lonely and deserted. Nha Be is innocuous now, almost unnoticeable at this point in time, its history unknown to most; to the majority of the locals, it's just another storage area. Nha Be is a different place now than it once was, when it played such an important role in what is recognized now as being a wholly futile endeavor.

In 1969, Nha Be was a sortie port for hundreds of navy river operations. It was an ugly and wholly utilitarian place lacking any semblance of beauty, but was our refuge from killing and/or being killed. We would

17. Nha Be

leave Nha Be along the Soi Rap, move along a few connecting tributaries, and then travel up the Vam Co Tay and Vam Co Dong to the Cambodian border, for up to 2 weeks at a time. Sometimes we followed the remote-controlled river mine sweepers that were stationed there. The VC were notorious for setting up waterborne mines along many of the rivers leading to and from Saigon. We usually followed the mine sweepers at least part way up river before they were returned to the base.

Uniform patch worn by those attached to the Naval Support Activity base at Nha Be, home of the Mobile Riverine Force.

For me now, passing the site of Nha Be was an emotional rollercoaster. Remembrances flashed through my mind's eye, much as if through a movie kinescope machine. I saw in my distant past the boats that were damaged, shot at, and sunk, and the men who were bewildered, pissed off, wounded, maimed and killed. In addition to the mine sweepers, Nha Be was home-port to PBRs, LCMs, tango boats, alpha boats, and a few swift boats.

A little less than two years after I left Nha Be, the VC sabotaged the base, and it went up in flames, decimating the entire area and closing the once bustling base forever. Its demise was a harbinger of things to come, as South Vietnam fell shortly afterwards.

Memories flooded back of nights spent there in the barracks, doing and smoking strange things, thinking strange thoughts. Escaping! Drug use, for me, was strictly limited to smoking marijuana, which was readily available, and of truly excellent quality. I was never a big drinker, but still needed something to occasionally take my mind off the present. Opium and heroin were available, but totally out of the question, and alcohol was never something that I enjoyed or could acquire a taste for. Riding the rivers was unnerving, to say the least, and an occasional attitude adjustment was just the thing to help put nature and some of life's better happenings into the forefront of one's thoughts.

We lived in the barracks when we were not out on patrol. My locker was filled with my new tools of employment: an M-16 light machine gun, which was the standard issue military weapon; an M-79 grenade single-

Remote-controlled river minesweepers tied up at the pier area at Nha Be. They preceded the river boats up river for a ways before returning, as most mines were set close to the river bases.

shot launcher; and a long-barreled .38 special with a western-style leather holster that I had inherited from someone who was leaving. I became very good with the M-79, which became more and more accurate as I learned to estimate distances better. It had a three-hundred-yard range, with a sliding sight that allowed the tilt of the weapon to vary the arc of the expended round, depending on the desired distance one wanted the grenade to travel. Being able to closely estimate distances became a very important talent to gain if one wanted to become proficient with the M-79. I loved wearing the .38. It was different from anything that the military

17. Nha Be

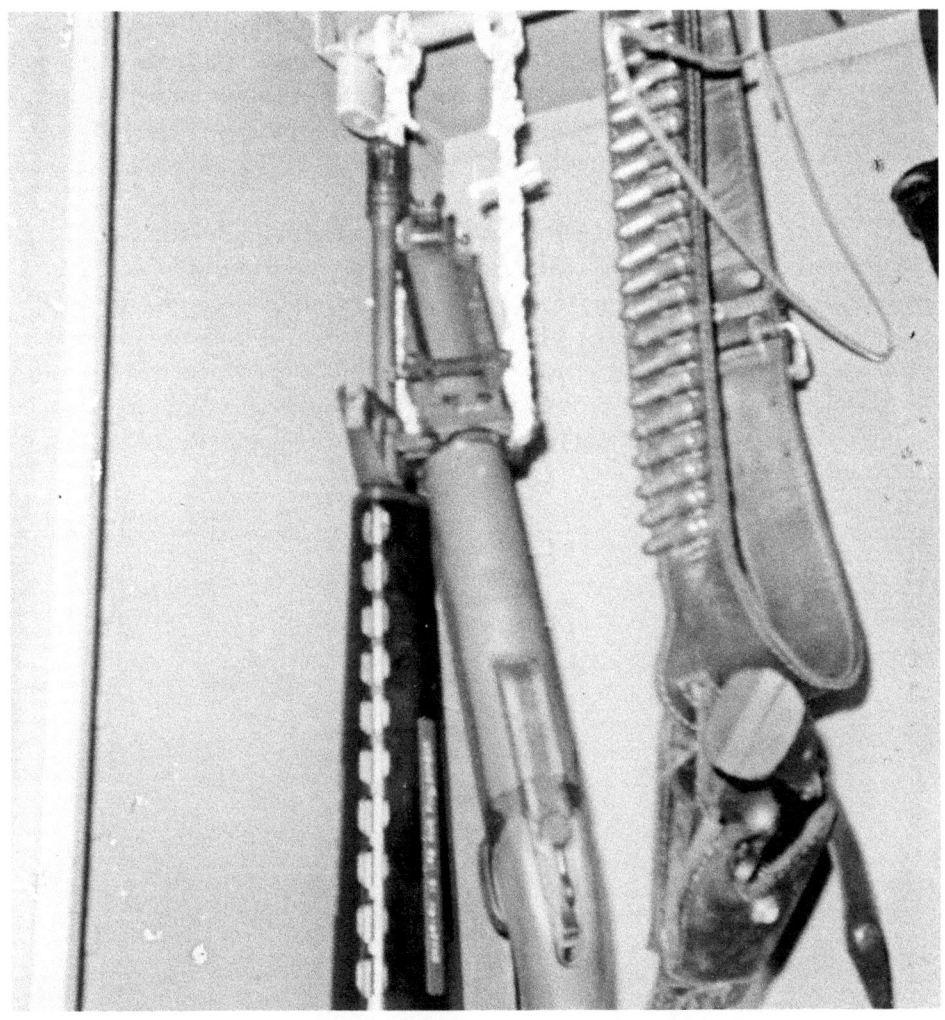

My locker in the barracks containing my personal weapons: a standard issue M-16 light machine gun, a single shot M-79 40mm grenade launcher, and a Colt .38-caliber revolver in a western style leather holster and belt.

would normally issue, and it was much easier to handle than schlepping an M-16 around town when we were back at Nha Be. We had to be armed at all times, and the .38 left both of my hands free. Wearing that pistol kept me flashing back to when I was a kid playing cowboys and Indians with my friends. I even had a leather tie-down strap secured around my thigh, like a real cowboy of the old west. I practiced my quick-draw and eventually became better than mediocre.

We wore shirts made of towels as we cruised down the rivers. We folded a towel in half, cut a head hole in the middle, and tied the sides together with a string. These towel-shirts absorbed the sweat better than our fatigues, and kept us cooler in the heat and humidity of the jungle. I don't know who first thought of the towel thing, but it certainly worked out great.

I had one other off-the-wall weapon that I had acquired from another sailor who was leaving Vietnam. He passed it down to me, as he could not take it with him. Attempting to take your weapon home with you was frowned upon by the Navy. It was a World War II vintage, .30-caliber, fully automatic M-2 carbine, with a couple of thirty-round clips. It had a sawed-off barrel and stock and a canvas sling that extended long enough for me to wear over my shoulder and fire it from just above my hip. I used it often.

Me on the stern of my LCM-8, dressed in fatigue pants and a shirt made of a folded towel, armed with my Colt .38 revolver.

A few of the crewmen of some of the river boats stationed in Nha Be, taking in a few brews at the enlisted club before going back out on the rivers.

It wasn't very accurate, but machine guns don't have to be very accurate in order to be effective ... and besides, it looked really cool.

We usually hung around the base, or the Enlisted Men's Club, drinking beer or playing nickel slot machines until it was time to go out on patrol or run supplies up to the ATSBs.

Each boat crew was responsible for loading our own boats with the supplies that we were to deliver, but not responsible for unloading them at their destinations. That was the job of the ATSB personnel.

As the *Angkor* sailed past and Nha Be disappeared off her stern, I smiled at another thought. The base was the home of 10- and 20-cent drinks in the club. It was the home of quick meetings between boats going out on patrol, and boats returning from patrol. There was actually a town outside the gates, full of bars and prostitutes ... a mainstay in every Navy town in the world. Nha Be was a center of commotion and traffic, and sex and booze and drugs. It was a place to forget, right on the river between the South China Sea and the port of Saigon.

I had an "encounter" one night with one of the lovely ladies of Nha Be. After all, we weren't always on patrol, and occasionally, basic human needs had to be met. It was a lovely experience for the few hours that it lasted. But, alas, two days later, after waking up and heading for the bathroom to wash, brush my teeth and take care of nature's call, I stood in front of the urinal, and when I began, I felt a pain like I had never felt before in my life. It was as if a "certain" part of my body was on fire. I screamed out loud, and immediately headed for the infirmary. After a few very invasive and embarrassing tests, I was told by the doctor that I had what the military referred to as nonspecific urethritis (NSU). Well, let me tell you something, there wasn't anything "nonspecific" about this. I knew exactly where it was. They shot me up with an antibiotic, gave me some pills, and in a few very uncomfortable days, the NSU was gone. They told me that, fortunately, I would have no residual effects from this encounter. It basically turned into one more of my personal learning experiences. I learned that abstinence would be an advantageous road to follow for the rest of my time here, and besides, masturbation has one obvious advantage over dallying with "nonspecific" partners: you don't have to look your best.

While stationed in Nha Be, one of my sisters contacted the Secretary of State of the State of Florida, Mr. Tom Adams, and asked him how she could obtain a state flag that her brother could fly on his river boat in Vietnam. Many of the river boats flew state flags or other flags that the individual boat captain had decided upon. One of the boats flew a skull and crossbones. The captain did this until he found out that the Viet Cong looked at that as an evil omen, and would pick that particular boat as the first to be attacked when cruising up the rivers. We saw very few skull and crossbones after that information became common knowledge. But state flags were numerous on the rivers, with most states being represented. I eventually received a letter and a flag from Mr. Adams, and flew that flag on every boat that I captained.

One could stand or sit on the docks in Nha Be, and watch a procession of hundreds of boats and ships of all types parade up and down the river twenty-four hours a day. Our security boats, manned by two-person crews, patrolled the dock area constantly in sixteen-foot Boston Whalers, armed

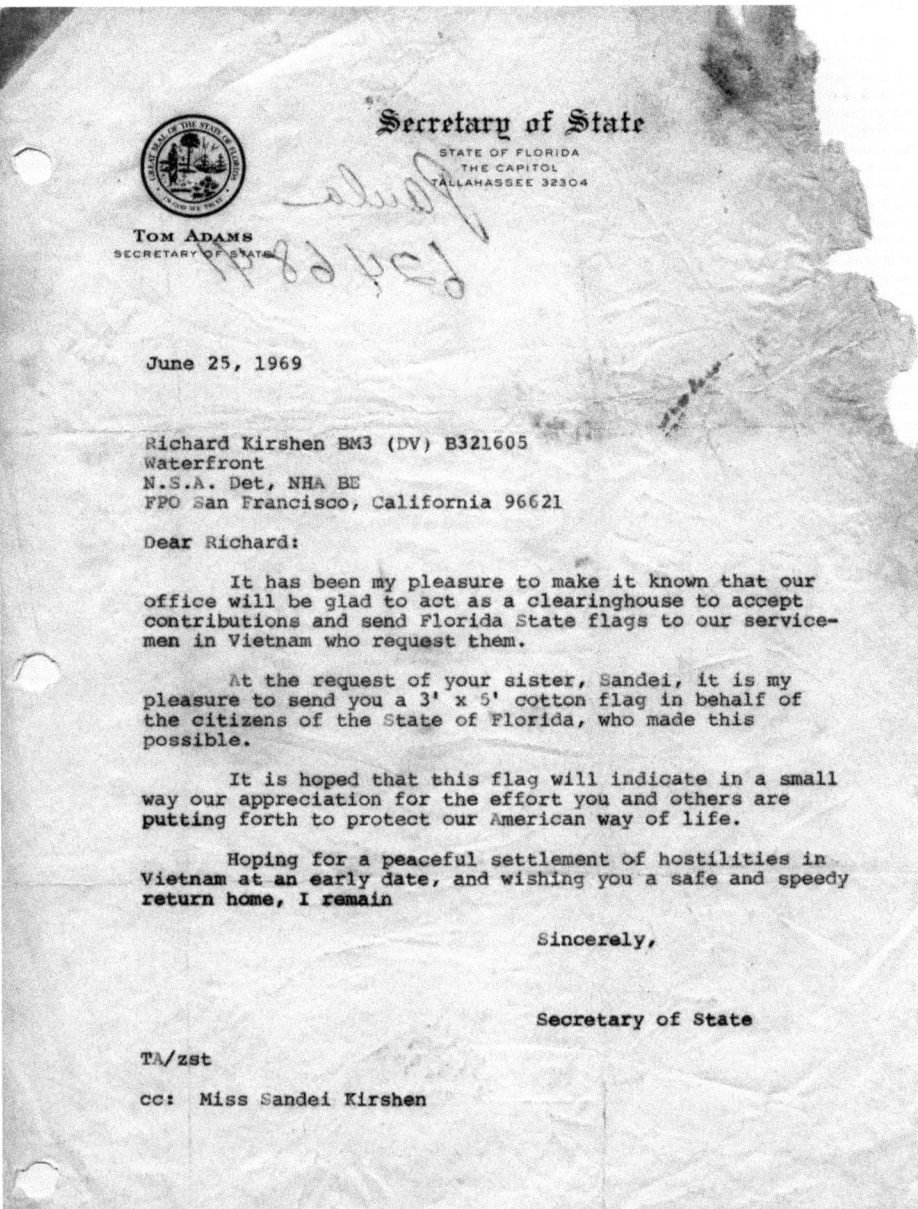

The letter from Tom Adams, the Secretary of State of the State of Florida, that accompanied a Florida state flag, which was flown from my river boat.

with .30-caliber machine guns, with a one hundred-twenty-five horsepower Mercury outboard engine. They rode back and forth, back and forth, all day, all night, 24/7/365, trying to keep the riffraff out. Surely, I shall never stumble upon Nha Be again.

18

River Jobs

Advanced Tactical Support Bases (ATSBs) were temporary floating Navy river bases, intermittently dotted along the Vam Co Tay and Vam Co Dong Rivers, all the way to the Cambodian border. We delivered supplies to these bases. Some of them were a three- or four-day ride up-river from Nha Be. They each had their own support staff and a contingent of patrol boats attached to them.

Sometimes we loaded, then transported Army troops, with their supplies and arms, and dropped them off up-river at their "Area of Operation" (AO), to do their Army thing. I did not envy their job. They had to trek through the jungle and swamps, carrying their own food and ammo in backpacks that must have weighed fifty pounds or more. In addition, they lugged heavy weapons and helmets and jackets. I thought that I was much better off letting my boat carry everything. I never had to wear a backpack, or tote a heavy machine gun with its required links of ammo. Their main advantage was that they could hide behind trees. You can't hide a boat in the middle of a river.

We spent nights tied up at the ATSBs, as the rivers did not belong to us at night. They belonged to the Viet Cong (VC), and the SEAL teams, and any of the numerous other Special Ops groups that operated in this area. One of those was the Phoenix Program, which was a joint CIA/military project tasked around the identification and elimination of civilian supporters of the VC. Another was the Military Assistance Command, Vietnam-Studies and Observations Group (MACV-SOG), which was a highly classified unit that conducted covert unconventional warfare operations during the war, both in Vietnam and in cross-border "situations" in Laos and Cambodia. Also involved in these special operations was the Army's 5th Special Forces Group (who dated back to World War II), which provided a defensive stand against the North Vietnamese Army and Viet Cong units based in Cambodia.

Troops and supplies loaded in my LCM-6 boat preparing for me to ferry them up-river to their destination. We could carry almost 100 fully armed troops in that boat.

Occasionally, I drove a boat for the SEAL team out of Nha Be, and dropped them off in what was referred to as the Rung Sat Special Zone. It was an area reserved for those freaky "Special Ops" guys. The Rung Sat was part of the Sac Forest, and referred to as the "Forest of Assassins." It consisted of four hundred and eighty square miles of tidal mangrove swamp, approximately twenty-two miles south-southwest of Saigon. It comprised over three thousand miles of interlocking streams and small rivers, so it was very difficult terrain.

Beginning in 1965, the U.S. Air Force began Operation Ranch Hand, which attempted to chemically defoliate the Rung Sat region by the use

18. River Jobs

The Army medic sits among the troops and supplies that we transport up-river to their area of operation. Our boat crew has no idea as to what their mission is; we merely get them there.

of Agent Orange, which, they hoped, would deprive the VC of food and vegetative cover. Agent Orange was a highly toxic chemical defoliant and herbicide manufactured specifically for the U.S. Department of Defense by both Monsanto and Dow Chemical Company. It got its name from the orange striped barrels in which it was shipped. Those involved in Operation Ranch Hand had a motto: "Only You Can Prevent a Forest." After dropping over twenty million gallons of defoliants and herbicides over rural areas of South Vietnam, their motto rang true.

The SEALs had their own boat. It was a modified LCM-6, with a 105MM howitzer cannon mounted on a flat deck that was constructed

Ferrying troops and supplies up-river to their intended destination, where I dropped them off and went back for more.

above the well deck. I never got to use that gun. I only got to drive the boat to drop them off, and to pick them up again whenever they demanded. SEAL Team One was in Nha Be.

SEAL Teams were instituted in 1962, and in 1966 the first team arrived in Nha Be to conduct direct action missions and to help train the Lein Doc Nguio Nhia (the Vietnamese SEALs).

Insignia patch worn by the members of the South Vietnamese Navy SEAL Teams, trained by our military.

Top: The SEAL team boat, which I drove for them, leaving them off in the early evening, and picking them up early the next morning after they did whatever it is that SEAL teams do. *Bottom:* One of my crewmembers showing the only way of bathing while up-river. It wasn't really clean, but it was refreshing in the normally oppressive heat.

This is how we lived while up-river: exposed to the elements and bugs. No protection from the sun or rain, and hammocks are not what they pretend to be … comfortable. Ever try to turn over in a hammock?

The SEALs operated in 12-man teams, broken up into 2 six-man squads. They were never assigned permanently to Vietnam, but rather on a six-month rotating schedule. They carried out day and night ambushes, preferring nighttime forays. They were used for hit-and-run raids, reconnaissance patrols, intelligence gathering, and psychological operations (psy-ops). Those operations were to instill fear into the enemy. The Viet Cong referred to them as the "men with green faces" because of the camouflage they wore. The VC did fear them, and often put bounties on their heads. The SEALs eventually accounted for 700 to 900 confirmed kills.

18. River Jobs

When "up river," we slept on our boats, in hammocks stretched across the well-deck, or on cots, out in the open, exposed to the elements. It rained constantly, and the rivers were full of flying bugs, leeches, and other nuisances, like bullets, bombs and rockets. It was hot and humid. We got, at best, intermittent sleep the majority of the time, with a full night's sleep reserved only for those times that we returned to Nha Be for a few days where we had the luxury of doors, and roofs, and air conditioning.

19

THE MEKONG

The *Angkor* continued to steam down the Saigon River until we reached a turn-off canal that headed east. It was a much smaller river, more like what I constantly navigated and patrolled while here on my own river boat. Without this man-made canal, boats would have to go all the way to the South China Sea to get to the Mekong from Saigon, an extra fifty or sixty miles. We passed hundreds of boats, loaded with rice, bamboo, sugar cane, sand, and a host of other products to be used or sold. Some came within a few feet of us as we traveled the sometimes tightly constricted waterway.

Finally, the canal met the mighty Mekong, and the *Angkor* turned

One of the thousands of colorful boats carrying an array of cargo, heading off the Mekong, along a connecting canal, and onto the Saigon River, into Saigon.

19. The Mekong

A river scene along the connecting canal from the Saigon River to the Mekong. Without this canal, and extra 60 to 80 miles would have to be sailed in order to get to the Mekong from Saigon.

north. The Mekong River is huge, varying from one to two miles wide at some points, with all manner and size of boats heading in every direction. It is a gargantuan waterway. I felt inspired to recreate Leonardo DiCaprio's "king of the world" scene in *Titanic*.

Lunch was served at 12:30, and once again, it was a meal beyond my expectations. I opted for the fish and chips, which was made from freshly caught fish and accompanied by locally grown vegetables. The chef-concocted batter had some exotic herbs and spices that I had never experienced before, and none of them were the seemingly ever-present cinnamon. Along with the salad bar and huge array of breads, it was a wonderful meal.

After lunch we continued steaming north, taking in the sights, interrupted only by a couple of very educational lectures by Mark, and an abbreviated history of Vietnam and the Mekong River by Long. They explained how important to everyday life the river was to the 60,000,000 people who lived along its banks, depending on it for food, water, and transportation. It was 2,700 miles long, beginning at its source high in the Tibetan or Himalayan Plateau, and running through China's Yunan Province, Myanmar (which used to be Burma), Laos, Thailand, Cambodia, and Vietnam, where it emptied into the South China Sea through the

Me at the bow of the *Angkor*, doing my best Leonardo DiCaprio imitation from *Titanic*.

Mekong Delta. The name was derived from the Thai, *Mae Nam Khong*, which translates to "The Mother of Water." The Mekong Basin is the second-richest area of biodiversity in the world, exceeded only by the Amazon. People have been living along its banks since 200 BC, and the first European to encounter the river was the Portuguese explorer Antonio De Faria, in 1540.

The Mekong met the Ruak River at the point where Myanmar, Laos, and Thailand converge. This was the famous Golden Triangle, where the drug trade was king, and poppies ruled all. The Mekong is the twelfth-longest river in the entire world. Our speakers, Mark and Long, held my interest and the interest of all those present for the extent of their lectures.

Dinnertime came and went, with another excellent meal. The next scheduled shipboard event was a movie in the dining room: *Good Morning, Vietnam*, with Robin Williams as the DJ Adrian Cronauer. It is based on a true story, and is a terrific movie with a fantastic soundtrack; but I had just watched it last week at home, so I skipped it and hung out on the deck watching and remembering. After the movie, I got Mary, and we retired for the evening. I fell into a somewhat restless sleep, waking numerous times, but finally getting some rest. Riding on the river today, with the wide range of passengers here on the *Angkor*, and encountering Nha Be for the first time in 40 years, brought up many long-forgotten memories.

20

THE ESKIMO

The boat crews that traveled the rivers during the war, much like the passengers on the *Angkor*, were also a disparate lot, encompassing all of the geographic, ethnic, and religious diversities of men and boys that the U.S. had to offer. Before they came here they were Southern rednecks, West Coast surfers, bikers, blacks, Latinos, Filipinos, Mexicans, Italians, Catholics, Jews, Baptists, Yankees, and rebels. After a short time, though, they all just became "River Rats." Friendships formed between men that, back home, would never have existed; would never have been allowed to exist. We became blind to both inherent and obvious differences. We just tried to keep each other alive. We trusted each other; we had to. Each boat had a captain, and three or four crewmen, including one who was in charge of the engines, and two or three crew members whose foremost job was helping the captain and engineman with anything that needed to be done. All were gunners, with specific assignments and specific weapons, whenever a firefight broke out, and we had to go to general quarters.

One of the more memorable crew members was a full-blooded Eskimo named Ila (EE-la), from an Inuit village in the north of Alaska. Ila didn't have to be there, as Native Americans were exempt from the draft. He was a stockily built, short kid, with coal-black hair, café au lait skin, thick eyebrows, and a rounded face. Ila didn't talk much and just did what he was instructed to do. He never gave anyone a problem. He was not on my boat, but on another boat in my river unit, so I did run into him upon occasion. On one trip up river we were the second of four boats, and Ila was in the third boat of the convoy.

One of the primary orders of operation that we were given by the heads of the river divisions was that (and I am paraphrasing here) when engaged by the enemy, we were to immediately return fire, put the boat in all-ahead-full mode, and get as much distance between us and the fire-

20. The Eskimo

zone as quickly as we could. As soon as this was accomplished, we were to use our radios to report our exact position, and call for air support. Under no circumstances were we to turn our bows into the oncoming fire and "duke it out" with the enemy. The reasons for this were understandable, twofold, and based on simple logic. We never knew how many were in the attacking party, or what weapons they had at their disposal. That information was always obscured by the jungle, and our boats could not hope to outfight a tank or any heavy artillery that might be hidden there. For all we knew, it could be an entire North Vietnamese Army (NVA) regiment concealed in the bush. We riverine warfare participants rarely, if ever, got to see the enemy that we encountered.

As our convoy of four boats continued our journey, we came to a bend in the river, and just as the fourth boat made the turn, all hell broke loose. We began taking heavy fire from the starboard side jungle. I heard the familiar sounds of AK-47s firing, bullets pinging off our metal boat, and witnessed smoke from B-40 rockets drift out of the heavy riverbank's vegetation.

My crew immediately began firing back, as did the crews of the rest of the boats. I was in all-ahead-full mode before the boat in front of me, and I almost passed him in my zeal to vacate the area. I was off quicker than a taffeta gown on prom night at the sound of that first shot. I looked back to see how the other boats were doing, and I saw the number three boat, Ila's boat, captained by a Texan named Jerry, turn toward the jungle and head directly into the gunfire.

We were about two hundred yards behind them now, but could see the action taking place. I was bewildered at Jerry's actions, and couldn't imagine what he was thinking. As I stared at this inexplicable drama playing out behind me, I could make out clearly what was happening aboard his boat. Only nanoseconds after the boat had turned toward the incoming fire, I saw the Eskimo sprint the length of the boat and jump up onto the afterdeck, in a move that would now be referred to as "parkour." We watched as he leaped onto the raised afterdeck, moved swiftly to the four-foot-high armor plating around the wheelhouse, confronted the captain, and stuck the barrel of his M-16 directly into Jerry's mouth. I watched in awe. I could see Ila say something to Jerry, but could not hear anything from this distance. All I did know at this point was that Jerry's boat had turned from its original perpendicular course, facing the jungle and gunfire, back to the parallel course down the river, faster than a man loses his self-esteem at a Lamaze class.

Some time later, after talking to some of Jerry's other crew members,

I became privy to the somewhat one-sided conversation between Jerry and the Eskimo. I say one-sided because Jerry couldn't talk very well with his mouth full. Evidently, immediately following the M-16's entry into Jerry's mouth, Ila had said very quickly, and very loudly, "I'm going to count to three, and this boat better be heading back up the river or we will never find your fucking head ... 1!—2!" ... but in that instant before he reached 3, the boat miraculously turned and resumed its original course up-river.

A few days later, when we returned to our home base, Jerry lost his boat. Well, he didn't actually lose it, he knew where it was, but when it went out again, Jerry wasn't on it, and it had a new captain.

21

VISITS ALONG THE RIVER

It was Christmas morning on the *Angkor*, and we awoke around 5:30. We climbed the ladder to the upper deck of the ship to check our e-mail. That was the only deck where Wi-Fi was available, and reception was

Guests on the *Angkor* lounging around on the upper deck, watching the river and river inhabitants pass by. This was the only deck where Wi-Fi was available on the *Angkor*.

This is the dining room on the *Angkor*, where meal after fantastic meal was served by the attentive staff, after being prepared by the ship's gourmet chef.

intermittent, at best, the farther up river we went. That limited Wi-Fi availability was by design, as the cruise company did not want people sitting in their rooms all day reading e-mail and checking out Facebook to see when their "best friends forever" (BFFs) fed their cats, or cut their hair, or went to the bathroom.

A great breakfast was available, with an omelet station, assorted fruits, meats, breads, cereals, yogurt, and just about anything else you could want for a morning meal.

At 8:30 sharp, a sampan tied up alongside of us and took us all into Cai Be. A sampan is a usually flat-bottomed wooden boat, available in many different sizes. Cai Be was a riverfront city containing floating markets, floating restaurants, and hundreds of boats carrying multitudes of diverse products in and out of the harbor. We pulled into a dock of sorts, and debarked for a walk through a rice paper factory, a rice wine factory, and a candy factory. All of them were in full production mode; all were lacking air conditioning. Some things never change. From there, we visited a French Gothic Catholic cathedral. After the church, we took a tour of

21. Visits Along the River

One of our day trips took us to the riverside city of Cai Be, where we encountered this French Gothic church. It was very much out of place in this city of mostly ramshackle huts and floating homes.

An operating brick kiln in Cai Be. These bricks are used to make most of the homes in the area. The kilns get up to 800 degrees inside.

Opposite, top: An exterior shot of the An Kiet house in Cai Be. One of the few extravagant homes we visited, owned by a local businessman. *Opposite, bottom:* An interior shot of the An Kiet house, showing its unusual, for this area, splendor and ornateness, definitely a rarity in this part of the country.

Kiln-fired bricks and tiles ready for use as construction material and for roofing implements.

what our guide said was a "traditional" Mekong Delta house. The An Kiet House, though, was by no means a traditional house in this part of the world.

The house was huge and ornate, on a large piece of property with fruit trees, and inundated with perfectly trimmed, multicolored bougainvillea. It was obviously owned by people of great means, compared to the abject poverty surrounding us. It was very much removed from the other 99 percent of the houses, shacks, and hovels we passed along the river. It would be like comparing Beverly Hills, with its mansions and estates, to Watts, in South Los Angeles, with its mostly ramshackle housing, and calling Beverly Hills "the norm." After the tour, we boarded our sampan, and returned to our ship for another outrageous lunch. There were always three or four choices for the noon meal.

After eating, we returned to town on the sampan and went through a brick factory. We were shown how the clay was formed into bricks, and fired in the huge dome-shaped kilns in 800-degree wood-stoked heat. They were in operation as we watched, and the heat was intense.

21. Visits Along the River

We walked from there into town and visited a candy factory, consisting entirely of coconut candy, as the Vietnamese weren't into chocolate. I can only assume that was because there is little refrigeration and air conditioning in this mostly tropical country, and a Hershey bar would not last longer than maybe four minutes before turning to a liquid mess, or a chocolate shooter. We all wrapped a boa constrictor around our bodies for a few photo ops, which seemed to be "the" tourist activity to do when visiting this factory.

We then headed for a tour of the house that was owned by the character in the 1992 movie *The Lover*, which was to be shown later on the ship. *The Lover* was based on an autobiographical novel by Marguerite Duras, detailing the highly illicit and scandalous affair between a teenage French girl (the author) and an older Chinese man, in 1929 French Indochina.

Even now, as it was in the late 1960s, the Vietnamese are a very industrial people. When I was here before, I noticed how everyone worked

A fellow passenger and I sharing the loving touch of a large boa at one of the tourist stops, which happened to be a candy factory in Cai Be.

One of my crewmates and I attempting to sell our LCM-6 boat. Before any buyers could be found, the Navy shut down our entrepreneurial attempt.

either fishing, or rice farming, or making something. My own entrepreneurial instincts arose once on my previous foray into Vietnam, when one of my crewmen and I attempted, unsuccessfully, to sell our river boat. It's not that we didn't have offers, but you know the military and how they cherished their toys. Selling military goods by anyone other than an authorized agent was strictly prohibited by those making a huge profit from those deals. Our commanding officer failed to see the humor in our venture, and we were instructed to take her off the market immediately. Those guys were always finding ways to take the fun out of war.

No one was idle, even during the middle of a war, which was probably why, after my first three weeks here in 1969, I came to realize that it didn't matter who eventually won the war. In either option, 98 percent of the people were still going to be rice farmers and fishermen for the rest of their lives. This would be whether they lived under communism or a so-called democratic ruler. In either case, the masses would most assuredly end up with a conniving heartless despot as a head of government, and their lives would not change even one iota. It just wouldn't matter. The only people affected by the outcome of that war were going to be the elite two percent who controlled the money, the government, and the land. Oh, yeah, I almost forgot ... and American corporations. Three weeks was all it took for me to decide that it was all a waste, and that people were dying for nothing. *What the hell was I really doing here, risking my life daily, and wasting others—for what?* The one time I asked a senior officer, "What are we doing here?" he responded with, "Your job, son ... your job." I just didn't get it, and no one could explain it, yet the war and the killing went on.

22

FISH FARMS AND WIPING OUT A VILLAGE

We were served another great dinner aboard the *Angkor*, and afterwards I felt a bit feverish and congested, so I took a few antihistamines and turned in early. I missed the movie, as I was in dreamland for the night.

We were up early the next morning. I was feeling much better, and the wonderfully diverse breakfast awaited us once again. After breakfast we had about forty-five minutes to kill before the sampan picked us up for our daily outing. The sampan was right on time, as usual. Everything on this trip so far was on time.

We headed to a floating home area, with thousands of homes floating on barges in the river. Please take notice of the television antennas on each floating home. In Vietnam, if your house floated, you were exempt from real estate taxes, since you were not using any real estate; hence, the abundance of tax-free abodes.

Most of those floating homes had cages beneath them, and they raised fish there. The majority of the tilapia in the U.S. came from those fish farms, as well as the catfish. There were literally hundreds of thousands of fish beneath each of these houses, and each house had a storage room reserved solely for bags of fish food. We watched their frenzy, as they were fed, which happened twice a day. It looked like the piranha scene in every movie you have ever seen about the Amazon.

From there we headed to a small canal that separated Vietnam from Cambodia. The canal was lined on each side by houses on stilts, with part of the house on land and part of the house supported by flimsy wooden poles sticking down into the river bed. I believe this has something to do with the lack of plumbing pipes, and toilets, as this set-up allowed all

22. Fish Farms and Wiping Out a Village

Top: Some of the thousands of floating homes along the Mekong River. Inhabitants of floating homes are exempt from real estate and property taxes. *Bottom:* An opening to the gargantuan fish storage areas below most of the floating homes. We were told that up to 150,000 fish were in these cages at any one time, and feeding time causes a frenzy.

Houses along the Mekong built part on land and part on stilts driven into the river bottom. Hanging over the river eliminates the necessity of plumbing pipes to take away the waste.

household waste and garbage to just drop into the river. Penned-in fish and duck ponds lined the river along both sides.

Once again, memories flooded back—memories of traveling the rivers long ago. One trip consisted of towing, alongside my LCM, a ninety-foot-long barge filled with close to a million pounds of sandbags. Those were going to be used up river at some of the ATSBs as fortifications. There was no sand up river in the jungle. The sandbags would be placed around the bases as protection from incoming fire and explosions. All the ATSBs were floating, but not all were anchored in the middle of the rivers. Some were tied up along the river banks to trees or stakes in the ground.

On trips like those, we were escorted by other boats, as our speed

Opposite, top: **Laundry day along the Mekong, with plenty of sunshine to dry the clothes, bed linens, and fishing nets.** *Opposite, bottom:* **Penned-in duck pond. Simple sticks with netting keep the ducks readily available as a food source.**

22. Fish Farms and Wiping Out a Village 123

was almost nil while towing, and we were sitting ducks on the river. The heavily armed escort boats were a great comfort to us as we plodded along at a not-so-swift 3 or 4 knots. A knot is an abbreviation of "nautical mile," which is equivalent to approximately 1.15 mile, a nautical mile being 2,000 yards. The enemy was a great deal more reluctant to attack a convoy of boats that were escorting a slower boat, than to attack the one slow-moving towboat.

It was not an easy task to pull a million pounds up river alongside one's boat. The current sometimes took over, and we would lose control of the boat. This happened to me at one point. I lost control, and my boat swept into the housing supports of one of the many villages along the bank of the river. The houses began to tumble as supports snapped like twigs. By the time I had regained control, I had decimated an entire village, just dumping them into the river. I had disrupted their lives, and caused great hardship and loss to those people who had so little. It was disheartening, and even at 20, and in those out of the ordinary circumstances, I felt the guilt of what I had done.

I imagined somebody flattening my parents' home, dumping all their worldly possessions into a fast-moving river where they could never be retrieved, and how that would make me feel. I imagined how it would make them feel; what it would do to their lives and how they would manage to cope with the loss. Those people lived in mortal danger on a daily basis, and I had made an already ghastly situation even worse. My crew chided me about it, even though they knew it was beyond my control. Telling me, "I can't believe you just wiped out an entire village by yourself. We're putting you in for a medal." It was very demoralizing, and I thought about it the rest of the day, as we wended our way slowly up river. I still think about it, and what long-lasting effects it had on the villagers.

23

CAMBODIA AND NIGHT TRAVEL

We continued our tour of Cai Be, visiting a Buddhist temple, where, oddly enough, the Weinstein bar mitzvah was taking place. We left after the appetizers (kidding). It was a nice temple, but by this point, I've been a bit over-templed. The buildings are nice, the people are nice, the robes are nice, but religion is just not my thing. I never trusted it. I never saw the point. I tried never to get involved with it. With that being said, the temples were absolutely gorgeous, some dating back a thousand years or more.

After the temple, we walked through town, past many food and goods booths, and eventually back to the sampan, and the *Angkor*. I couldn't bring myself to buy or eat anything from a fruit, vegetable, or mystery meat vendor. It's not exactly the South Miami Beach Food Festival. I didn't want some exotic foreign parasite taking up residency somewhere in my body, just so I could have the pleasure of experiencing lemon grass or some other such locally grown delicacy.

Upon returning to the ship, we thanked Long, our Vietnamese tour guide, and said goodbye. He is not allowed into Cambodia. Actually, he is allowed into Cambodia, but he cannot work there. When we got to the border, we would pick up a Cambodian guide.

The *Angkor* steamed on until we reached the Cambodian border, where we stopped and tied up to another ship that was anchored in the middle of the river. It took about two hours to clear customs. I didn't understand that, as this ship made two passes a week through this area, and the Cambodian customs agents should know the *Angkor* by now. It's not like they check all sixteen staterooms and look for contraband or anything; they just hang out. I don't get it. I guess it's just a money thing.

Entrance to one of the throngs of Buddhist temples along the Mekong in Cambodia, some over a thousand years old.

23. Cambodia and Night Travel

One of the larger Buddhist temples along the river, housing a monastery, living quarters for the monks who see to the temple.

During this lull, Cousin Steve informed the crew that he was having a problem with the air conditioner in his room, and within ten minutes the crew snapped into action ... and brought him two bottles of hair conditioner. There was obviously a communication problem, but it did show just how attentive to any rising "crisis" the crew really was, and how well prepared they were to deal with any inconvenience or emergency that might occur on the cruise.

Also, during this interval, the crew entertained us with a fruit carving exhibition. I think that if you are really good at fruit carving, there is something lacking in the rest of your life. Either that or you just have too much spare time. But it was somewhat enlightening, and in their own way, they are superb artists, so I just let it be, and feigned interest.

After this more than rude interruption by the Cambodians, we steamed onward and the river got darker. Cambodia by night, compared to Vietnam, is like being in the far reaches of outer space, with very few lights along the banks of the river, and far less river traffic. It appeared as if electricity was not as prevalent in the outer reaches of Cambodia as it was in Vietnam. It was pitch-black; one could not differentiate between where the river ended and the bank began. It was like being in a sealed cave. This was the second-darkest place I have ever been. The all-encompassing darkness did make the sky different, though: so many stars, like I had never seen before. The heavens were littered with twinkling lights, with barely a space between them. So far, though, Cambodia was a dark, barren, sparsely populated place.

A few hours later, we saw the glow of city lights ahead of us. It was Phnom Penh, the capital and largest city in Cambodia, off in the distance lighting up the sky. We anchored a couple of miles downriver from the harbor entrance for the night and had another fabulous dinner.

Dinner was followed by a showing of *The Killing Fields*, the movie about the incursion and occupation of Cambodia by the Khmer Rouge in 1975. The brutality and inhumanity depicted was unimaginable, helping to create a night full of vividly gruesome images. I'm sure that most Americans do not recall this extraordinary time in the world's history. It was just one more instance where the majority of the world turned its back on an ongoing atrocity, and looked the other way, as unspeakable evil was unleashed on part of mankind. That movie, and its implications, made the night even darker.

My previous trips up these rivers, during the war, were similar. The nights were also pitch black, but far more frightening. We didn't travel often after sunset, but sometimes it was necessary. Remember, the night belonged to "Charley."

On one occasion, the crew and I were spending the night at an ATSB in Tuyen Nhon (Too-ee Non), on the Vam Co Tay, just shy of the Cambodian border. The base commander had received intelligence that the area was being surrounded by VC, and an attack appeared imminent. That news was confirmed by sightings through night-vision glasses, and the base went to general quarters. You could actually see, off in the woods, the VC amassing around the perimeter. Much of the jungle around the base had been cleared. It was just bare, open fields for a couple of hundred yards in every direction around the base, until the woods and jungle flourished once again. That was done to prevent the enemy from sneaking up on the camp unnoticed. As a general rule of thumb, during wartime, it was always much better if the enemy snuck up on you while being noticed.

My boat and crew were not attached officially to that base. We were just passing through, so we decided not to stay for the upcoming confrontation and fireworks. In a very enlightened moment, I had surmised that the fewer times you involved yourself in a firefight, the less your chances of actually being shot. It seemed quite logical to me, a real no-brainer. My crew wholeheartedly agreed, even though it meant a night ride on the river. I informed the base commander that we were heading out; he approved, as air support would be in soon, and it wasn't like we were needed. Sometimes it's good not to be needed.

Off we went, into the ebony night, slowly, very slowly. We could barely see the river, or its twists and turns. Some parts of the river were so narrow that at night we could not keep from running into overhanging branches and tree limbs. It was like driving through onyx. There were lights nowhere. That was the darkest place I had ever been in my life. Our intensity level was at a peak, as we had to keep constant watch as to where we were going, in our barely effective attempts to see ahead of us.

The smaller rivers and tributaries were the worst, even during daylight hours. Some only gave us fifteen to twenty yards of leeway on either side of our beam, just enough room to turn around our eighty-foot-long LCM, although due to the flat bottom, and the independently operated twin screws (propellers), those boats were very maneuverable. I could move that boat a matter of inches in any direction. I could turn it completely around in its own length, spinning on its invisible axis. Without the wheel, and using only the engines, I could maneuver the boat into or out of almost any location. I became very good, and my crew acknowledged and appreciated that talent.

On those rivers, both fear and awareness were omnipresent. The fear was obvious and expected, but your degree of alertness took on a whole different dimension; one's sensory awareness skyrocketed to new levels. Your eyes endlessly searched the river banks, from side to side, for anything visual that seemed out of the ordinary. You noticed a leaf blowing in the breeze or a riffling frond, as your eyes explored the empty spaces in the foliage for any horizontal movement, or the glint of shiny objects. Your ears could recognize the sound of one bird, over the noise of countless other birds and animals, and then move on to the next noise ... and the next. It was like listening to a rock band and keying in solely on the drums, then the keyboard, then the lead guitar, hearing each individual sound distinctly amid the entirety of the band. Your nose could smell the jungle ... and what was not jungle. You could pick up the scent of a suspended pot, cooking rice over an open flame ... and you could smell death.

I have learned that that awareness level never leaves you, once you have experienced it. If you doubt me, ask anyone who has ever encountered combat. You are acutely aware of your surroundings for the rest of your life. You always know what is going on in that twenty-foot circle around you. You know what and who is there, and you can read the "threat level," if it exists. This ability to "become one" with your immediate environment becomes instinctual. I count it as one of life's attributes.

One of the smaller rivers we were forced to traverse, offering little in the way of protection from ambush from either or both sides. There was barely room to turn around in some of them.

As we put space between ourselves and Tuyen Nhon, we could see the lights of the firefight behind us, with frequent rocket flashes, and lines of tracer rounds. Tracer rounds are bullets that are manufactured with a small amount of pyrotechnic charges in their base. They are ignited by the burning gunpowder after being fired. The charge burns very brightly, making the round visible to the naked eye as it speeds through the air. That enabled the shooter to see where he shot and gave him the ability to make aiming corrections. In most machine guns, there is a tracer situated every fifth round in the magazine. We could hear the loud explosions and sound of gunfire, and we could smell the gunpowder. Once again, all of our senses were coming into play. Helicopters were lighting up the night sky, as their rockets sped downward and the red tracer lines from their mini-guns and M-60s littered the surrounding woods.

We moved on stealthily, at a snail's pace, down the river, back toward Nha Be, peering into the sheer blackness. Hours later, after our intense efforts to keep the boat between the invisible banks of the river, the sun began to rise. Vision returned, and we sped up and ran full throttle all the way to Nha Be, and relative safety.

My eyes were strained from trying to see in the dark. They ached. I couldn't adjust to that kind of shadowy murk. My brain was tired. I slept for 16 hours.

24

Phnom Penh and the Killing Fields

The next morning, the *Angkor* steamed into Phnom Penh and tied up to a wharf, instead of the usual anchorage. After another sumptuous breakfast we departed for our first excursion of the day.

Phnom Penh's home of the Cambodian kings. As ornate and jewel encrusted as anyone's home ought to be.

24. Phnom Penh and the Killing Fields

We were off to the grounds of the Royal Palace, a venue that proved once again that Mel Brooks was right: "It's good to be the King." The palace was a magnificent piece of property containing numerous gold- and silver-appointed buildings and edifices. Those came from the collections and constructions of the many Cambodian kings of the past. Included in the numerous displays were tons of gold, silver, diamonds and emeralds. Nice digs, even for a king.

In the mid-seventies, King Norodom Sihanouk, along with his family and aides, was detained for four years under house arrest. That was during the bleak and vicious days of the Khmer Rouge incursion, led by Pol Pot. Anyone who tried to escape the palace was quite unceremoniously beheaded—or maybe ceremoniously, as I am not thoroughly familiar with beheading protocol. After the palace tour, we returned to the *Angkor* for lunch and a short rest, and then it was off to the actual "killing fields."

Khmer Rouge was the more common name of the Communist Party of Kampuchia (CPK). They took complete control of Cambodia on April 17, 1975, and viciously ruled until January of 1979. They attempted to implement new social engineering policies by instituting agricultural reform throughout the country. It was an utterly disastrous failure. We were taken to a specific location, a few miles out of town, where the Khmer murdered over 20,000 Cambodians. Four Khmer Rouge executioners murdered 20,000 people ... four ... think about that for a minute. The mass graves were dug up only recently to expose the horrors of that place.

No bullets were used in these executions, as the philosophy of the Khmer Rouge was that no life was worth the cost of even a single bullet. Clubs, trees, bare hands, and saw toothed fronds from palms were used to beat, club,

One of the many mass graves throughout Cambodia. A sick reminder of the occupation of the Khmer Rouge, and the millions who died at their hands.

Top: **The exterior of the Monument to the Dead, containing thousands of skulls of the poor unfortunates who met their fate at the hands of the Khmer Rouge.**
Bottom: **The interior of the Monument to the Dead, showing some of the carnage caused by the Khmer Rouge during their reign.**

strangle, slit the throats, and decapitate the thousands of victims. A monument building was erected on this sight. It is four stories high, with the center being a square glass container holding all of the excavated skulls and bones from the scores upon scores of innocents who were murdered there.

24. Phnom Penh and the Killing Fields

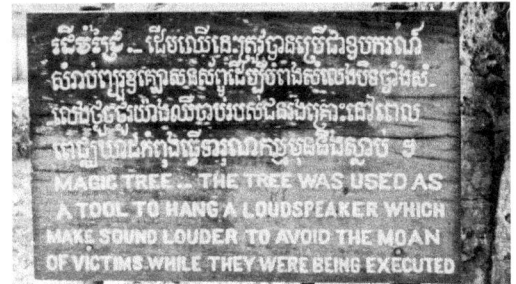

Above: One of the most vile spots in Cambodia, and possibly the world: the tree upon which the Khmer Rouge killed children by smashing their heads against it until they were dead. *Top, right:* The magic tree, whose hanging audio speakers were used to drown out the pitiful moans and screams of those being executed.

Men, women, and children, it just didn't matter to the Khmer Rouge. They even had a large tree that was used to beat children's heads against, until they were dead. One has to wonder what state of mind a person had to be in, in order to do something like that. *What can he possibly be thinking? How can he justify it in his own mind?* It is just such a nonhuman thing to do. I didn't get it.

That was a very moving excursion into yet another memorable place; memorable, once again, for all the wrong reasons. As with my visits to other similar localities, there was only silence from the throngs of visitors who slowly wandered through. It appeared that, unfortunately, the world was full of those quiet introspective places where, over time, untold horrors had come to pass. Places that took the words away from people. Places that allowed you but a mere glimpse into what really went on. Places where unsuspecting visitors can only look, and think what it must have been like ... and why it was allowed to happen. Places rife with the ghosts of evil.

From there we were off to even one more very "up" locale, the Tuol Sleng (Hill of Poisonous Trees) Genocide Museum in Phnom Penh. It was situated on the grounds of S-21. S-21 was a former high school that was converted, in August of 1975, into a torture and execution center by the Khmer Rouge. That was only one of approximately one hundred and fifty execution sites set up around the country. Of the seventeen thousand people imprisoned at Tuol Sleng, there were only twelve known survivors. That was a .0007 percent survival rate; absolutely unbelievable.

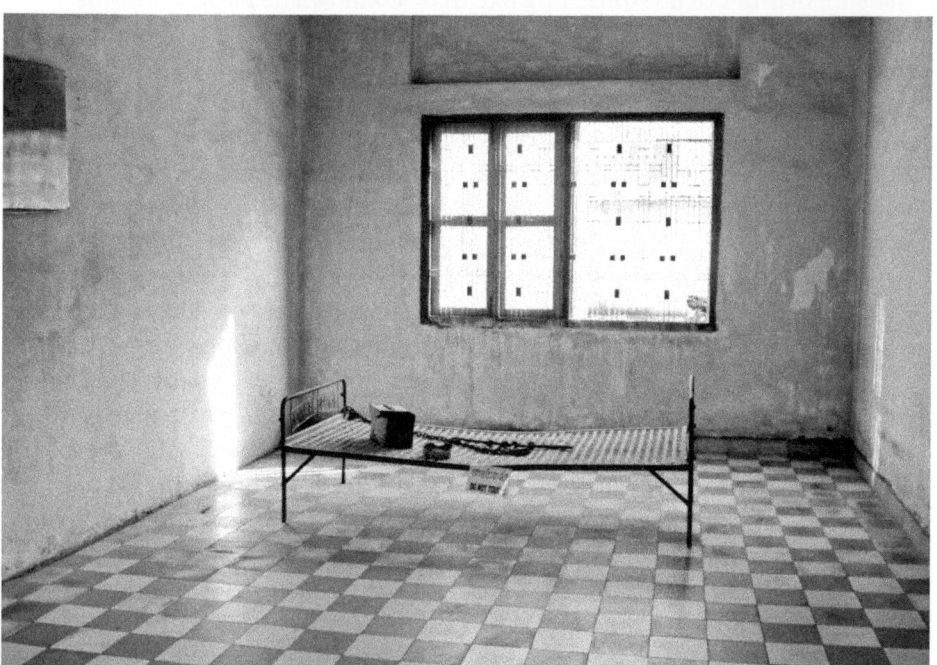

24. Phnom Penh and the Killing Fields

THE SECURITY OF REGULATION

1. you must answer accordingly to my questions - Don't turn them away.
2. Don't try to hide the facts by making pretexts this and that You are strictly prohibited to contest me.
3. Don't be fool for you are a chap who dare to thwart the revolution.
4. you must immediately answer my questions without wasting time to reflect.
5. Don't tell me either about your immoralities or the essence of the revolution.
6. While getting lashes or electrification you must not cry at all
7. Do nothing, sit still and wait for my orders. If there is no order, keep quiet. when I ask you to do something, you must do it right away without protesting.
8. Don't make pretext about Kampuchea Krom in order to hide your secret or traitor.
9. If you don't follow all the above rules, you shall get many lashes of electric wire.
10. If you disobey any point of my regulations you shall get either ten lashes or five shocks of electric discharge.

The sign that all inhabitants had to heed explaining the regulations of security at the genocide center. Read them slowly and take them in, and think about the psychological effect of such material on the unfortunates.

Opposite, top: In one of the rooms of Tuol Sleng Genocide Museum, pictures of hundreds of the dead souls who passed through this hell hole are displayed, in hopes that nothing like this will ever happen again. *Opposite, bottom:* The interior of one of the rooms at Tuol Sleng. This room was used exclusively as a torture room for the unfortunates. Bare and simple ... if only the walls could talk.

The Khmer were mainly concerned with anyone who had prior connections with the former government of Cambodia, or any foreign government, as well as professionals and intellectuals. Those people were the first to be eliminated. All others were moved from the cities to the countryside to fend for themselves. They had to grow what they needed to survive and provide for their own medical care. Thousands starved, or died of minor infections, injuries, and curable diseases. Many were indoctrinated, tortured, and killed at S-21. Meticulous records were kept by the perpetrators of this wickedness and immorality. The pictures of the dead and dying, and of cells used expressly for torture, were chilling. The Khmer Rouge posted rules for the detainees at the genocide center, and these were to be strictly adhered to by the unfortunate souls who ended up here.

There are so many different ways to torture people, to kill people, to humiliate and degrade people. It was almost endless what the depraved mind could conjure up. The Khmer Rouge was a malignant tumor that infected a small sliver of the world, a totally amoral assortment of evildoers whose minds were twisted by even more twisted leaders. They murdered and tortured children, and much like the Holocaust of World War II, and the Armenian genocide of 1915, perpetrated by the Turks, the world stood by and watched or ignored as over two and a half million people were eradicated. This was almost half the population of Cambodia at the time.

Vietnamese troops fought their way into Cambodia in December of 1978 and captured Phnom Penh on January 7, 1979. The despotic Khmer leaders fled to Thailand and China, finally ending their reign of terror, but not before leaving the country littered with millions of secreted, unexploded land mines. Those devices are still killing people. "Inhuman" is the best I can do to describe the actions of the Khmer Rouge.

25

OUR PRISONER

As a riverine warfare participant, I only witnessed the results of man's inhumanity to man a few times; you know, things over and above "regular" killing. I came across a number of decapitated corpses among the many floating bodies we encountered on the rivers. Bodies bloated and turned black when left in the water, and the smell of death was something one never forgot. I was also confronted by bodies hanging from tree limbs that jutted across the river, and dead bodies strewn along the banks.

We captured just one enemy combatant during my 9-month stint on the rivers. He was a sniper who fired at our boat just before the river took a sharp right turn. I think he must have missed a chapter in "sniper school"—the chapter about watching what happens to your intended prey after you miss your shot at him.

My engineman, John, told me that he had seen where the shot originated from and that we should pull into the side of the river and go after the shooter. I told John we never leave the boat. "Never leave your boat, unless it's not floating," was one of our basic directives upon becoming a riverine warfare participant. Of course, there were a few exceptions to that rule, such as a fire on the boat or if you are sinking, or if you happened upon a five-star restaurant up-river somewhere (which never happened).

John was quite persuasive, though, and I gave in. It sounded exciting. For a few minutes I could pretend I was a Marine or a real soldier. We pulled into the river bank and tied off to a tree. John and I each grabbed an M-16 and some rope, and headed into the jungle. We left Dale and Dennis aboard to guard the boat.

As we came to where John thought he had seen the sniper, we saw him climbing down the tree that he had been holed up in. His back was to us, his rifle slung loosely over his shoulder. We got the drop on him

Me holding the AK-47 we captured from an enemy combatant. Standard issue rifle for the North Vietnamese Army units.

and could have shot him and killed him right there. No one would have known ... but we didn't.

John held his weapon on our prisoner as I tied him up. Remember, we were in the Navy, and knots were a strong point with us. I secured his hands behind his back with a figure-eight knot acting as very serviceable handcuffs, and led him back to our eagerly awaiting crewmembers. They were shocked and astounded that we had actually captured someone. A captured prisoner was quite a rarity for a sailor. That was our most personal encounter with the enemy. Killing in the jungle was typically highly impersonal, as you rarely saw the person you killed.

25. Our Prisoner

We drove up river for another hour before we came to a village, and tied the boat up along the bank. The village was about a quarter of a mile from the river, along a dirt path through very dense jungle. As John and I walked the prisoner in front of us, I told John, "Listen, if this guy runs for it, you shoot him." John said, "Fuck you, I'm not shooting anyone in the back." I said, "Look, I'm the boat captain, you shoot him." And on we squabbled, about who was going to shoot this guy, as if quibbling over which of us was going to mow the lawn or take out the garbage. If the prisoner had understood any English at all, he would have been long gone into the jungle. We eventually turned him over to the local military post, and headed back to the boat. We kept his AK-47. It had a bayonet on it, which I had never encountered before.

Only after continuing up river for a while did I momentarily wonder what they were going to do with him, or to him. I didn't think about it for very long. Basically, I just didn't care.

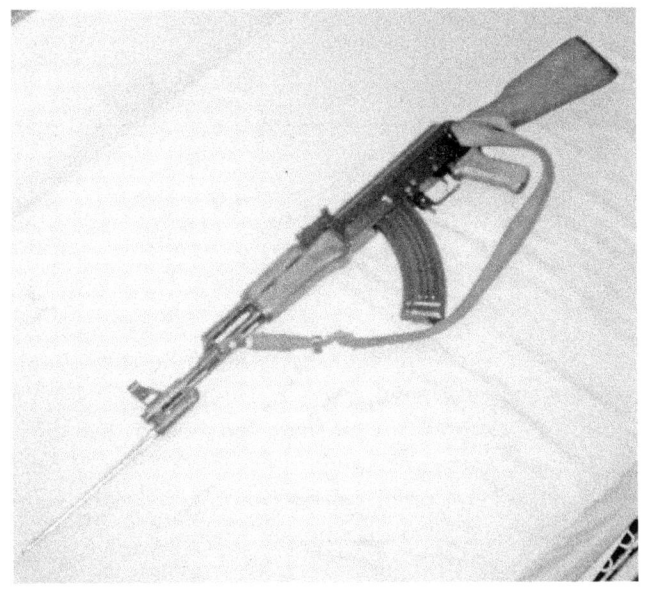

Displaying the AK-47 on my cot in the barracks at Nha Be. It was kind of rare for those of us on riverboats to capture anyone or anything.

26

THE BOAT SHOW

After the uplifting experiences at the killing fields and the Genocide Museum we had a silent, pensive bus ride back to the ship. We were all in need of rest and refuge, from both the oppressive heat and the vile images. Everyone sought out relaxation and reflection. I sought my personal relaxation and reflection in a few Jack Daniels and rocks. Unfortunately, or maybe fortunately, I had a few too many, too fast. I'm not a big drinker, but the buzz felt great, and I was now definitely relaxed and the images of the past few hours were waning.

Before dinner was served, a show was performed on the cleared-out main deck. Included was a Cambodian band consisting of a steel drum, a

Beautiful young Cambodian dancers from the local orphanage who earn a living by dancing native dances for visitors from all over the world.

One of the female dancers being accompanied by the young male "monkey dancers" who portray the movements of monkeys along with the women dancers in the Cambodian Monkey Dance.

kind of xylophone, and one multi-stringed instrument of unknown origin. The music was accompanied by the exotically refined and graceful gyrations of three exquisite young Cambodian female dancers. Their movements were serpentine, fluid and sinuous. Also dancing were young boys performing what they referred to as "monkey dancing." They wore monkey masks and moved like monkeys to the rhythmic beats of the accompanying band.

After this presentation, the girls and the faux monkeys got together and did the "bamboo dance." That consisted of the beautiful young girls

One of our ship's passengers attempting the Bamboo Dance with one of the Cambodian dancers, as others from the dance group move bamboo poles back and forth at an ever-increasing rate.

jumping through two parallel bamboo poles, which were being snapped together and apart just off the floor to the beat of the band's music, by the assisting monkey boys. The speed of the snapping poles kept escalating and the chance of the girls' ankles being crushed increased with each upbeat of the music. The girls then got volunteers from the audience to join them, and taught them the dance. Our young girl passengers held their own, and hardly broke any ankle bones at all.

Dinner was served, and after the meal, I was still a bit too wasted to go out. Mary, Steve, and Debbie went into town on a tuk-tuk with a few of our shipmates. A tuk-tuk is a motor scooter pulling a four-person open cab behind it. They went to the Foreign Correspondents Club (FCC) for a few drinks. The FCC was a famous rooftop bar, where most of the news people gathered during the Khmer Rouge incursion, until they were ordered to leave. The Khmer Rouge wanted no witnesses or accounts of their actions.

Even though this day started out somewhat depressing, the beautiful dancers and the show they produced brought everyone's spirits back up and made one and all feel better. It was a pleasant ending to a day of diverse activities. I slept through the night, not even aware of Mary's return.

27

NEW LIFE

There were a few of those "pleasant" endings when I was here during the war—days that ended on a rather high note. One might get the idea, from most of the previous references, that everything that occurred to me, or those around me, during the war was either horrific or life threatening. That certainly was not the case. There were brighter, happier, more enlightening moments—moments that were still frightening, dangerous, and thought provoking, but in another way.

While stationed in Cam Ranh Bay, I was a Landing Craft, Mechanized-6 (LCM-6) boat captain. An LCM is the boat you see in all the World War II movies that involved amphibious landings on a beach, where the soldiers run off the front onto the beach after the ramp is dropped. My chief function was to transport the local Vietnamese who worked at the Cam Ranh Bay Naval Support Facility (NSF) to and from their village each day. Those were the cooks, gardeners, painters, and housekeepers, all of the jobs deemed too menial for regular Navy guys. The few who spoke English worked in the PX or the enlisted club.

It was a forty-five to sixty-minute ride from the base, across the wide expanse of picturesque Cam Ranh Bay, to the small village of Bagnoi (Bah-Noy). I did this twice a day, every other week, just me and one crew member. We alternated weeks with another boat crew. Roughly fifty workers were carried on each trip. Our morning run was at 5:30 a.m. and the evening run, to return the workers to their village, was at 5:00 p.m. In the interim hours I was the designated base diver, doing odd diving jobs in the bay or in the areas surrounding the bay, up and down the central coast of Vietnam.

One day around three in the afternoon, I was summoned to the base infirmary. When I arrived, I was greeted by a Navy doctor, who informed me that he wanted me to take a young, pregnant Vietnamese woman across

27. New Life

the bay to her village. He said that it was time for her to stop working at the base. "Don't worry," he said, "she was not due for at least another two weeks."

I was told to take the Lighter, Amphibious Resupply Cargo (LARC), which was a huge, balloon-tired, amphibious truck/boat. A "lighter" is an open barge or boat used to load or unload ships offshore, or to transport goods for short distances in shallow water. I was one of only two men on the base certified to operate it.

I looked around for someone to go with me, as a crewman. The only guy I could find who wasn't otherwise occupied was a sailor named Chuck. He was a bit inebriated from hanging around the Enlisted Club all afternoon, but he was available. It seemed like a simple trip: drive the young lady across the bay, up onto the makeshift road, over to the village medical hut, then return. What could go wrong?

Chuck and I helped the young mother-to-be up onto the LARC and headed down to the waterfront. I drove off the road, over the beach, into the water and switched the controls into marine mode. This allowed the propellers to turn, instead of the rear wheels, and slowly, the three of us headed across the bay. A LARC's top speed in the water was close to seven knots, as opposed to my LCM, which could do slightly more than double that speed.

About a quarter of the way across the bay, I noticed that Chuck was either passed out, or sleeping, on the front seat next to me. The young lady was reclining on the rear seat. Suddenly she reached up and tapped me on the shoulder. I turned around and her pretty, coffee-colored, almond-shaped eyes stared into mine. In soft broken English, she said to me, "Baby come now." That was something that no one had ever said to me before. Well, not without a comma after the first word. I was at a loss; I didn't know how to respond, so I initially ignored her. She was determined and quite motivated, though, and tapped me once again on the shoulder. This time, she said in a bit louder, more informative voice, "BABY COME **NOW**!!"

OK, I admit it: I was stumped. I had no idea as to what to do, or how to react to this situation. So I shook Chuck awake. As he approached consciousness, he looked at me through his Scotch-induced stupor. I said matter-of-factly, but with a slight air of authority, being the boat captain and all, "Chuck, go deliver this girl's baby." Chuck squinted his eyes, smirked, and told me to go fuck myself. I said, "Hey, I'm the boat captain. Go deliver the baby." He then explained to me, with somewhat slurred speech, that he should drive the boat, and I should deliver the baby, because he was in no condition to do anything that "technical." I saw that this was not getting us anywhere, and I could sense that the young lady was becoming a bit impatient with our bickering, so I relinquished the helm to Chuck and climbed into the back seat. She was a couple of years younger than me, about seventeen or eighteen, and very slightly built, like most Vietnamese, except for her cantaloupe-sized belly.

I looked around for some blankets, or towels, or anything soft (they always do that in the movies), but all I could find were orange kapok life vests. I spread some out on the aluminum seat and helped her lie down. She laid her head back on two more of the vests that I had propped up as a makeshift pillow. I reached under her and, without her protesting, slid her black pants off, then her panties, and positioned one more life jacket under her butt.

She somehow got across to me, using mostly body language and hand gestures, that she had one child already, and assured me that she had a good idea as to what was supposed to happen. I think that was what she was trying to tell me. I hoped that was what she was trying to tell me. I was counting on her guidance. I lifted one of her legs up on the top of the seat back, and the other over the seat onto the floor. I positioned myself between her splayed legs ... and, together, we waited. She started to have what I learned later were contractions. I held her hand and stared expectantly between her legs, which at that point was still a very appealing sight.

Soon, though, her teeth gritted, her eyes closed tightly, and she squeezed my hand hard, much harder than I would have thought her small delicate hands were capable of. I watched her push. Low guttural moans emanated from deep within her. Her breathing came in short gasps. A short time later, I saw something happening. I saw the top of a baby's head, or what I presumed and wished was a baby's head. Then I thought, *You idiot, of course it's a baby's head. What else could be in there?* I saw her stretch open. She stretched wide enough to make any man feel inferior. I couldn't take my eyes off her. It was amazing, creepy, and frightening, all at the same time. My mesmerized, trance-like state was shattered abruptly, though, when a gallon or so of some type of fluid squirted and oozed out of her, all over me and the life jackets. A couple of minutes or so after this, the baby's entire head made an appearance. It was like being in a National Geographic film. I knew enough to put my hands under the baby's head to catch it. She made another few grunting noises. Only moments later, the baby squirted out of her like a wet bar of soap out of a squeezing fist. I caught it. There was a great deal of blood and gooey stuff. Soon after

27. New Life

her initial expulsion (the baby), something else slid out of her, attached to the tube that emanated from the baby's belly.

Now, at that particular point in my life, I was completely unaware of the existence of placentas, as only the girls got to take "health" class in my high school. I thought something was going seriously wrong. Seemingly important parts were falling out of her. *Was I supposed to try to put them back in?* I screamed at Chuck, "Hey, what the hell is this?" He turned around, gazed into the back seat, held back a gag, and just said, "Oh, shit!"—then turned quickly around and continued driving the LARC.

I told Chuck to give me his shirt. Without argument, and without looking back again, he passed it to me over the seat. I wrapped the baby, and all of the extra parts, gently into the shirt, and handed the bundle to the mother. Chuck found a relatively clean rag in the front of the boat and tossed it back to me. I soaked it with some of the drinking water we had on the LARC and gently brushed it across the mother's forehead and face, and gave her a drink. I wet the rag again and took the baby from her. Very tenderly, and very softly, I cleansed the now crying baby as well as I could, and then handed her back to her mother. As she cuddled the baby, I cleaned up between the mother's legs and her thighs. She held the shirt-wrapped baby tightly as I washed her. When she was comparatively clean, I slid her panties and pants back on. I asked her if she was all right, using only international body language. I smiled, arched my eyebrows, spread my arms wide, with palms up, and slowly nodded my head, questioningly. She dazedly smiled back up at me, with pretty much the same dazed look that Chuck had exhibited earlier. How funny to find myself with two people buzzed in such totally different ways, for totally different reasons. Clutching her baby tightly to her chest, she smiled softly and nodded. I took that as a signal that she was ok, and as well as could be expected, under the circumstances.

About twenty minutes later, after I took the wheel again, we reached Bagnoi, and I drove the LARC out of the water, much to the shock and amazement of those locals who were nearby watching. They had never seen a truck come out of the water and head down the road. The new mother guided me to the local medical center. We dropped her off and she gave me a soft kiss on my cheek as she was carried away. We headed back to the base. Chuck was semiconscious all the way, mumbling something about me owing him a shirt. I was euphoric at the thought of new life, in a place where I had witnessed so many lives come to such an abrupt and violent end. Yes, that was truly one of the "up" days.

28

Visiting a Cambodian Village

We awakened at 6:30 a.m., once again to a perfect day aboard the *Angkor*. The temperature was in the low nineties, with mid-sixties humidity, and clear, azure skies. After breakfast, the ship departed Phnom Penh and headed up river for about forty-five minutes. We tied up in Prek Bang Kong, a small village northeast of Phnom Penh.

After disembarking, we were taken on a tour through the village, attempting to get a little insight as to how the average Cambodian lived. One of the houses we visited had a family of silk makers. The open, lower part of the house contained two looms, and a homemade bicycle wheel silk-spinning device of some sort. The women worked at those jobs for eight hours a day making silk fabric.

During that time, they produced roughly one meter of 54"-wide fabric. They did that daily until they got a roll of about 50 meters. They then started again on a new roll. Those women produced fabrics in a multitude of different colors and patterns. Some were standard, often-repeated designs, and others were custom loomed for specific clientele. It was tedious, repetitive work. Cambodia had no unions, or workman's comp, or Occupational Safety and Health Administration (OSHA) to look out for the well-being and welfare of its work force.

We went through the village market on the way back to the *Angkor* and everyone bought some scarves, bags, table runners, and a collection of other silk products. All were reasonably priced and the tourists were happy with their purchases. We returned to the boat around 10:30 a.m. and everyone just sat around and checked e-mail, or read, or just lay back and relaxed. Some took naps, and some of the more serious photographers on board took advantage of the many unusual photo ops that

28. Visiting a Cambodian Village   151

A Cambodian woman weaving silk on an ancient hand-operated loom situated under her stilt house.

A Cambodian woman spinning silk threads on a homemade spinning machine utilizing a bicycle wheel and other local products.

cropped up as we cruised along the river. All in all, it was a gorgeous morning.

After lunch, the ship tied up in Angkor Ban, home of another Buddhist monastery. We walked through the ornate temple area, populated by orange robe–clad Buddhist monks. They were setting up for some type of celebration.

28. Visiting a Cambodian Village

Our walk continued through the surrounding village and a few of us got quite up close and personal with some underweight Brahma bulls, as well as some of the pleasant village children. As we walked down the path through the village, two goats took an unnatural liking to Debbie, and followed her around. She pretended she was disturbed by this, but I spotted a twinkle in her eye that plainly showed she liked the personal goat-attention.

A pleasant, slow walk through the village returned us to the temple, where we heard music blaring from the loudspeakers. It was a most unexpected and surprising rendition of "House of the Rising Sun," by Eric Burdon and the Animals. When that song ended, a local singer took a mike and serenaded us with some traditional Cambodian songs on our walk back to the ship.

Orange-robed Buddhist monks praying inside the temple in Angkor Ban. Praying takes up a majority of the monks' everyday lives.

The ship got underway again, and a number of people got sick, showing signs of vomiting and diarrhea. Well, not actually showing, as we took their word for it. That was not something one had to see in order to believe. If most of you think back throughout your past, there were probably no instances where you asked someone to prove they were suffering from vomiting and/or diarrhea. There appeared to be a virus affecting some of the passengers.

Everyone who wasn't sick sat around the main deck, reading, writing, and watching the landscape glide by; everyone just took it easy as we steamed up river once again. Dinner was served, with many local fruits

Monks hanging out outside the monastery in Angkor Ban. Not everything is serious, as you can see the smile or laughter of the one monk.

and vegetables on the menu as well as local recipes for the main course. Those afflicted with whatever it was, did not partake in dinner that night, as they wanted to maintain proximity to a bathroom.

After dinner, a few stayed for the movie *The Quiet American*, with Michael Caine and Brendan Fraser. The movie was adapted from Graham

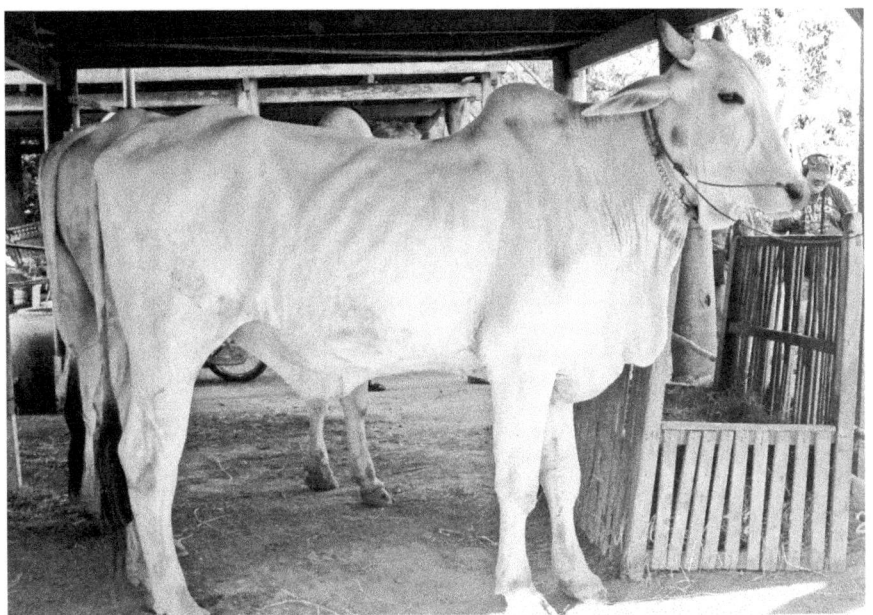

Top: One of the many brahma bulls we came across in one of the outlying villages near Angkor Ban. They are used for transportation purposes as well as field work in the agricultural regions. *Bottom:* Some of the beautiful young village children in the surrounding area of Angkor Ban. They were friendly and seemed happy, playing games and looking at the tourists.

A few of our ship's passengers walking through the village, being followed by some of the local goats. The goats followed them for over an hour as we walked the paths through the jungles.

Greene's 1955 antiwar novel, set in French Indochina in the early 1950s. The rest of the passengers called it a night after another good day on the river (for most of us). We were off to bed around 10:30. Well, actually, Mary fell asleep in the dining room while watching the movie, but I steered her back to the room, where we called it a night.

29

Again with the Darkness and My Night on the River

Like most of the ride through Cambodia, we never passed any large cities on the river on my last incursion into Southeast Asia those many years ago. My experiences on the river were limited to endless kilometers of jungle, small villages, and hamlets.

Most of those villages we saw were in various stages of ruin and chaos due to constant bombing by the U.S. and by attacks from the Viet Cong. It had been my observation that bombs caused a great deal of disrepair wherever they were utilized. War, in general, is not such a good thing for one's house ... or one's life.

There were no lights at all at night, other than intermittent cooking fires. This greatly limited our movement at that time. We normally tied up for the night at a village or one of the ATSBs. Actually, even if I had the chance to travel at night, I would not have. You could hardly make out the river in the black of night, and other than the previously mentioned trip, due to the attack on Tuyen Nhon, I rarely did. The rivers were a frightening place to be after sunset. At least, during daylight hours you could see the jungle and the banks of the river; at night ... nothing.

The only advantage I could see to traveling at night was that you could spot the enemy's tracer rounds coming at you, and you knew where to shoot back. But I'm not really sure that is an advantage. During the daylight hours we just shot into the jungle where we surmised the enemy was attacking. I only knew we had "made contact" when the enemy stopped firing.

One night we were hit simultaneously by two B-40 rockets right at the waterline. The boat filled with water and sank in a matter of minutes. My crew and I were blown off the boat in the explosion. We were cruising on the river, just finishing some C-rations, heading back to Nha Be and a quiet, restful night in a barracks. Then, bright lights, loud noises, gunfire, an explosion, and screaming; and now I was wet and treading water. *The boat's gone; somewhere on the bottom of the river where the current's dragging it. I have to swim; but which way? To which shore? It's too dark, I can't see.*

I had a headache. I was dizzy. My head was spinning. My body ached. There was no more river boat. There was nothing beneath my feet.

Damn, which way? I have to pick a way and get out of the water.

There were snakes, crocodiles, giant catfish so large that a grown man could stand upright in its open mouth, and khorat (huge fanged frogs). It was all coming back to me now: the orientation class about the rivers here in the Delta, just before they made me a boat captain. I remembered thinking, *Who cares about this? I'll always be on a boat.* They told us what to look out for; what, besides the enemy, was dangerous. I had to get out of the water and had to stay quiet. I didn't know what side of the river the enemy was on.

Oh, damn, mangroves, just like in the Keys.

They're great for the environment, but a bitch to climb out of. They didn't need any ground under them. They grew right in the water. They're so damned slimy and slippery. I couldn't seem to grasp anything. I needed to get out of the water. I had to get up onto dry land. My clothes were getting heavy. I couldn't tread water with my boots on anymore. My legs were aching. My arms were getting tired. My head hurt badly. I was starting to sink into the river. I had to grab something and pull myself up onto solid ground. *This is frightening. I seriously don't want to be here. I can't see much; too dark. My leg is stuck in a mangrove root. I can't move. I'll be here forever. There, free, out of the water.*

The darkness was punctuated only by the light of the tracer rounds, and now, with the water clearing out of my ears, I heard the gunfire. Different sounds now. Return fire. Some of our boats were still fighting. I recognized the sounds of the .50, and the M-60. *Shit, my boat is gone, with all my stuff on it.* Crawling now; on slimy, stinking mud with things cutting my fingers and my knees, away from the river. *I have to find dry land.*

I'm tired, I have to rest; I can't crawl anymore. Fear encompassed me like Dracula's cape. I shook. *How am I going to get out of this? Who the hell knows where I am … or even, if I am?* I heard noises in the jungle. *Oh shit, tell me it's not a tiger. I could get eaten by a fucking tiger and no one would ever know. Wait, maybe it's just a Saola* [a local deer type animal]

29. Again with the Darkness and My Night on the River

Mangroves growing on the sides of the rivers keeping us from seeing the enemy, and making it difficult to climb out of the river, if necessary.

or an ibis or crane walking around looking for food. I'm hoping for the deer.

OK, what do I have with me? Not much, just my knife, my wallet, a belt, my jungle boots. My wallet? What the hell do I need a wallet for, out here? Everything was wet and slimy. I had no food, no drinks; no survival

More of the dense mangrove growth along many of the rivers in SE Asia.

stuff. No gun or ammo. What did survival school teach me? *Find protective shelter and hide from the enemy if you think they may be close. Close? They just sank my freaking boat. Of course they're close. Should I seek higher ground? Hide in a tree, maybe? No, I could fall out. There could be snakes in the trees.*

29. Again with the Darkness and My Night on the River

I walked, crouched over, my eyes searched the darkness for anything recognizable. I moved slowly now, almost sloth-like, listening to every noise. I was totally aware of my surroundings, tuned into my environment. The jungle abounded with noises at night. I categorized them as either friendly or harmful. The ground was harder now, my boots squished, I had mud everywhere.

The situation was very distressing. This never happened to me back in Miami. Nothing there ever scared me. Thinking now, I can't remember ever being scared before I came here, to this nightmare of a place. Maybe just that one time I wrecked my dad's car while he was watching. But then again, I'd never been in a jungle before, surrounded by things that wanted to either eat me or just kill me. I sat under a tree and listened. The gunfire was dying down now. *Did we win? How many of our boats were sunk? Did anyone die? What the hell am I going to do?*

I heard voices, and strained to make them out. *Let it be English. Let it be a platoon of Army guys.* Damn, the singsong sounds of Vietnamese. I lay down and quickly pulled palm fronds over me. The voices got closer as the unseen speakers walked through the jungle. There were no sounds of machetes cutting anything. They must be on a path. I lay still. Insects were swarming me. There was buzzing in my ears, my nose, my eyes: gnats or flies, or who knows what else lived out here. Something crawled up my leg. The footsteps moved closer; sandals broke small branches and crackled on the dead fronds. The path was nearby. Like a marble statue, I lay motionless, barely breathing ... on the verge of screaming.

They passed by, whispering, walking one behind the other, only feet from where I was frozen in this humid, infested, wretched place. I didn't move, but I began to breathe again. My body lay motionless for hours, like a never-ending MRI, becoming a home to unseen mites and insects. I felt stings like the fire ants back in Florida. Things crawled across my face, and still I didn't move. Night encompassed all. The jungle truly was a dark room full of deadly objects. It was pitch black with barely a minimum of twinkling stars visible through the canopy of trees. I looked through a break in the vegetation covering me ... and then I attempted to sleep. The insects did not allow it.

Daylight: birds chirped; something large bellowed in the distance. I inched the fronds, slowly and carefully, from my face and moved my head back and forth furtively. I saw nothing; only golden strands of sunlight filtering through the trees. I listened, and heard nothing. I slid the vegetation away and stood up. The mud was dried and caked on me, protecting me from some of the insects as I had attempted to sleep. I brushed myself off and headed back toward the river. I smelled terrible. I wanted to wash everything off of me, but thought about the camouflage that the dried mud offered, and reconsidered. I sat on the bank of the river and waited.

I was thirsty and hungry. My neck and face itched. My body had been ravaged and abused. I was cut and bleeding. My head was throbbing. I was sure that I suffered at least a minor concussion in the boat explosion. I needed food, but most importantly, water. A man could survive about three days without water. *I won't drink the river water. The locals drink it; and bathe in it; and wash their clothes in it; and use it as a fucking toilet. Would I drink it as a last resort? Yes.*

After a few apprehensive hours, I heard engines, and hid behind a tree. The throaty roar of the diesel got closer and I saw small brown and green boats: PBRs, heading right for the oxbow in the river where I had secreted myself. As they closed in on my position, I waded out to waist-deep water, put my hands above my head and began waving and yelling. They saw me, and aimed all of their weapons at me. I yelled in English, and they closed in. I recognized the boat captain. We got here about two weeks apart. I exhaled loudly as he saw me and came in to pick me up. He barely recognized me, muddy and bloody, disheveled, arms and face covered with bites and open wounds.

We heading back to Nha Be, sated with water and C-rations, I learned that the other three on my boat had been picked up. Two were wounded, but no one died. I was presumed captured, dead, or lost and a search party was sent. On the way back, I went over my ordeal in my head; the gamut of emotions I ran through in such a relatively short time. The overriding emotion was fear. It was a fear of what nature had to offer in its basest form. But beyond nature, it was the fear of being alone that dominated; the fear of not being found.

30

THE FIGHTING MONKS

We arose early the next morning, around 6:30 a.m., to another gorgeous day. The ship headed for its terminus point on the Mekong, before turning back toward Phnom Penh, and continuing the rest of the cruise on the Ton Le Sap. We pulled in to Wat Han Chey, home of an 8th-century Buddhist monastery. It was a three-hundred-step climb up to the monastery from the river. Some passengers opted to take the bus that climbed the alternate road, but Mary and I did the climb. The temple was magnificent, as are most Buddhist temples, with monks abounding everywhere. One of the structures dated back over a thousand years ... and it looked it.

We entered one of the temple buildings and were greeted by the sounds of two monks reciting their mantras. I rank that right up there with Gregorian chants as far as interesting musical meditations are concerned. These guys are completely atonal and repetitive, offering a few high notes and a few low notes, but mostly sounding like the hum of an incorrectly installed ceiling fan, but that is how it is supposed to sound. They did this for hours, every day. This solidly reaffirmed my decision to never become a monk.

The views of the river from this lofty vantage point were spectacular. One could see the winding river for miles down below, and the numerous river islands that dotted the way. Walking slowly by myself around this huge compound, I was soon joined by two young Cambodian girls and one boy. The children introduced themselves, and accompanied me around the entire area, supplying a private guided tour of the monastery. I gave them each a dollar for their expert navigational skills and lively color commentary. They were very cute little things, probably no more than five or six years old. At the time, it didn't dawn on me that they should have been in school. That was one of the reasons that we were told not to

Passengers walking up the wooden steps from our ship to the monastery at Wat Han Chey. More like a long ramp than actual steps or stairs.

30. The Fighting Monks

Some of the same passengers returning to the ship on the same rickety wooden pathway down the side of the mountain.

tip young children we run into in our travels, as tipping discourages them from going to school. They would rather make a few bucks than attend classes; but I couldn't *not* tip them.

After inspecting the rest of the compound, we were given the option as to which way to descend back to the ship. All of the rest of the passengers decided on either the same stairway we had used to get up here, or the bus. I alone opted to walk down the sloping, semi-paved trail, through the woods, instead of the countless steps that I had climbed on the way

30. The Fighting Monks

Some of the child guides at the monastery at Wat Han Chey. They don't ask for "tips," but everyone slips them a few dollars.

Opposite: The last remaining piece of the original monastery at Wat Han Chey, which is over a thousand years old. Pieces of the new monastery are in the background.

The child guides posing in front of the beautiful view of the Mekong, far below the monastery.

up here, even though it meant a slightly longer walk. It was rather peaceful. I could hear small animals scurrying through the brush, and birds singing and chirping in the ancient old-growth forest that encircled the monastery. This was the first time I had been alone since this trip started. I walked slowly, savoring the rare few minutes of isolation and solitude in this very private, serene spot, ten thousand miles from home.

Partway down the trail, in front of an ornately colored and decorated outbuilding set back in the forest, I came upon a most unusual sight. I observed two monks in a heated argument. It got so heated, in fact, that they began pummeling each other with their fists. This might be the only picture in the world of two Buddhist monks fistfighting. I watched in astonishment as the two orange-robed holy men at first, verbally abused one another, and then proceeded to beat the hell (if monks actually contain

30. The Fighting Monks

any hell) out of each other. Fists were flying, robes were flailing, the afternoon sun was glistening off clean-shaven, bobbing and weaving heads, and voices were getting louder. I was fortunate enough to snap one picture of them hitting each other, so that my shipmates would not doubt my highly improbable story. That was a truly amazing sight. When they noticed me, they immediately stopped their struggle, and rapidly vacated the area.

I continued my serene, now memorable, walk down the path toward the *Angkor*. Everyone made it back to the boat, and after showing them my pictorial proof of the aforementioned fracas, they all asked me to e-mail them that picture. This photo was then voted, unanimously, as the "Picture of the Trip" so far.

The one and only fighting monks picture.

Lunch was served, and once again, the choices were all good. I had eaten an abundance of salad and fruit and other seemingly healthful foods on this trip and I felt great. The boat tied up later in the morning in Kampong Cham, home of another Buddhist monastery. I decided to forego the afternoon foray, as my entire perception of Buddhist monks, and Buddhism in general, as the "peaceful way," had been tarnished forever by the previously witnessed monk-scuffle. I'll never be able to look at a Buddhist monk in the same light again.

31

ZIPPO BOATS AND BODY COUNTS

The river narrowed noticeably as we neared Kampong Cham, summoning up thoughts, once again, of the rivers I toured on my boat during the war. Some of those rivers were fifty yards wide, or even less, with dense jungle growth on both sides. I think that is why we on the river boats were referred to as Target-Rich Environments (TREs) by the enemy. This term, TREs, first came to light in some captured VC documents that gave their perspective of us river warriors. We were "easy pickin's."

Anything or anyone hiding in the jungle, only yards from the banks of the river, was virtually hidden from view. That was why we hardly ever saw anyone who ambushed us. Maybe that's the reason they call it an ambush. "Ambush": an act or instance of attacking unexpectedly from a concealed position, from the Middle English (1250–1300), "enbuss," which meant literally "to set in the woods." Only the telltale signs of smoke from the guns or rocket launchers, as they opened fire on us, were evidence of their presence.

Sometimes, the smoke was caused by us, or more specifically, the Zippo boats. Zippo boats (as in the famous "Zippo" lighters) were river boats specially equipped with electronically fired napalm shooting cannons. Napalm is a mixture of a thickening or gelling agent, and gasoline or some other flammable liquid. Initially it was used against buildings, but later became an antipersonnel weapon. It was first developed at Harvard University in 1942 and its primary use was in incendiary attacks against Japanese towns and cities in World War II. For Vietnam, napalm was manufactured by Dow Chemical Company in Michigan.

The Zippo boats would aim at suspected enemy positions along the river banks and shoot flaming napalm into those spots. It not only burned

31. Zippo Boats and Body Counts

people to death, but also burned up all the oxygen in any given area and suffocated them. In addition, if the jelly-like substance did get on you, you could not get it off. It would just burn through your body. As you likely know, water boils at 212 degrees F. Napalm reaches 800 to 1200 degrees F. The effects of napalm are quite an ugly sight to behold. Remember earlier when I told you that events take place in war that could not take place under any other circumstances? Well, the use of napalm is one of those things. There are no other circumstances under which there could be any plausible use for napalm. Its only purpose is to kill and/or maim human beings. Except for the delivery system, it borders on being a medieval weapon.

From a quarter of a mile away, we could feel the heat. I didn't want to be any closer. I couldn't even envision what that must have been like ... to be on the receiving end. Probably somewhat akin to having kettles of hot oil poured on you, over the walls of a twelfth-century castle. The jungle was so thick that it was hard to imagine that anyone could even get to the river bank from the other side. We fired back, never knowing if we actually hit anyone, or killed anyone. The only hint that we had made any contact at all was if they stopped firing. Then, we just assumed we had hit our mark, and called in our fabricated, exaggerated body count numbers, to go along with everyone else's invented and inflated numbers. The powers that be wanted those body counts, but it was close to impossible to relay any truthful information regarding that facet of riverine warfare. We always had to make up numbers. It's not like we went back, slogged through the jungle, and counted dead, bullet-ridden or napalm-charred bodies. Once we were out of range of the enemy fire, we never went back ... never.

32

THE AFTERNOON TRIP WITHOUT ME

I decided to forego the afternoon outing today. Mary went, with most of our shipmates, to even one more Buddhist temple. The draw there was that this one was populated by hundreds of banana-eating monkeys. I didn't think that banana-eating monkeys were such a big deal. Monkeys and bananas have always gone together, like Buddhist monks and the color orange, or like bees and nectar. While the afternoon tour was away, an intense rainstorm hit. It was a veritable downpour, the first of the trip, and it cooled things down for a while. I hung out on the ship and relaxed. The outing group returned a bit damp, but all happy, smelling like bananas, and ready for the next event. The next event involved hanging around waiting for dinner, catching up on e-mails, and

Monkeys have free reign at most of the monasteries and eat the plentiful fruit that grows in and around all of the Buddhist gathering places.

32. The Afternoon Trip Without Me

Fishermen along the Mekong have not changed their boats or methods for a thousand years, with the exception of motors; same nets, same way of catching fish.

watching life on the river slowly flow by as we steamed back toward Phnom Penh.

I've decided that riding the river here was not much unlike what I perceived Lewis and Clark must have experienced in their travels in the 19th century through early America. If the corrugated steel abodes and thatch-roofed huts here were exchanged for tepees, the difference would be negligible. Small colorfully painted boats were tied up alongside the villages. Villagers rode out in the boats, tossed nets in their daily fish-seeking regimen, with all of the villagers sharing in the duties of daily life. Other than the boat's engines, not much difference at all between them and canoes.

Dinner came and went, and this was the first really mediocre meal since the beginning of this trip. The chicken was not very tasty, and there was something in the recipe that I believe was supposed to be a bit softer than small pieces of .06-gauge wire, but unfortunately was not. I'll blame it on undercooked lemon grass. Oh, well; one not-so-good meal among many great meals is not such a terrible thing to have to endure.

After dinner we all hung out and spotted the intermittent lights and

Most of the fishermen's boats are just dugouts, carved out of a single tree, but some are painted in bright colors, not much unlike early Native American boats used a half a world away.

boats on the river, until the spectacular nighttime view of Phnom Penh once again came into view. Glittering like a neon oasis in the desert, it filled the night sky as we entered the port. We slowly cruised through and past the city, under the modern bridge across the Ton Le Sap River. Later, as the lights of the city faded off our stern, we were once again thrust into the ebony world of the river at night. The ship anchored, and the crew put on a native dance exhibition, incorporating the passengers, who, try as they might, just didn't have the dexterous finger or hip abilities of the crew. It was quite an interesting and entertaining exhibition.

The crew's dance was followed by the movie *The Lady*, the powerful story of Su Kyi, who in 1990, was won election as the leader of Burma (now Myanmar). The military thwarted her efforts to take power, though, and kept her under house arrest for more than a decade. She became the first Asian woman to win the Nobel Peace Prize. It was an interesting story, to end another great day on the river, made even more memorable by my surprising encounter with the fighting monks.

33

R & R

The U.S. Military Command in Vietnam, back in 1969, made sure that everyone involved in the Vietnam War also encountered a few "great days." They came up with what they called the "Rest and Recuperation Program," or R & R. Technically, R & R was a five-day break from the duties of war, which did not count against the annual thirty-day leave, which was afforded all military personnel in the war zone.

The special feature of R & R was the fact that the U.S. government would fly the recipient, absolutely free, to his choice of ten world-class cities, and then, after his five days of freedom, fly him back to the war zone. The five days did not begin until the plane touched down in one of those cities. Those included Hong Kong, Bangkok, Honolulu, Tokyo, Taipei, Singapore, Manila, Penang (Malaysia), Kuala Lumpur (Malaysia), and Sydney, although Honolulu was reserved only for those personnel meeting their wives. To provide this service, the government paid Pan Am Airlines and its subsidiaries twenty-three and a half million dollars a year.

A serviceman had to be "in-country" for a minimum of ninety days to be eligible for R & R, but he was encouraged to take it after six months so that it would break up the normal one-year tour of duty in the war zone. Space was allotted to each service in direct proportion to the number of men it had in Vietnam. This rate boiled down to 65 percent Army, 15 percent Marines, 12 percent Air Force, 6 percent land-based Navy (of which I was one), and 2 percent Coast Guard. Those serving on Navy and Coast Guard ships were not given R & R, as those ships rotated often. After ninety days in-country, each serviceman was given a "wish list," where he submitted his top choice of preferred time and city for his R & R. This did not always pan out as he wished, but by this time, most men did not care where they ended up, as long as it was away from Vietnam, and the war.

The local R & R centers in each city handed out brochures with little hints as to what to do and what not to do. A sample of what was in these brochures is the following, which came from Taipei: "Keep out of the buses, or you may lose your wallet. Do not purchase the company of a girl for more than 24 hours at a time; they seldom look as good in the morning."

The main gist of R & R boiled down to the single-minded pursuit of pleasure. This came in many forms. First of all, after living in the jungle for months, came good food, clean sheets, and hot water. Those things were mostly unavailable to the average soldier. The next objective was, obviously, female companionship. For this reason, Bangkok was a favorite destination. Petcahburi Road and Patbong Road, along the Golden Mile, offered the neon-lit Goldfinger Massage Parlor, the Whisky A Go-Go Club, and some 50,000 bar girls. Yes, that is not a typo ... 50,000 bar girls. Some unfortunate soldiers, though, found out that a small percentage of those girls were actually boys, which created some very awkward, albeit memorable, moments for those men. This female companionship, which in Bangkok usually included the ability to speak English among their many and varied other skills, could be secured for $11.00 a day or a slightly discounted, "one time only," special rate of $50.00 for the entire five days. Remember, this was 1969.

Other cities on the agenda offered similar but additional perks. Tokyo offered many more museums, cultural destinations, and cooler weather. Sydney offered surfing and "no-rice" meals, along with the sight and companionship of non–Asian women. Hong Kong was the shopper's paradise, or as it was known then, "The world's largest PX." Hawaii was a crowded destination because it was closest to the U.S. mainland and easiest for a meeting with one's wife or girlfriend.

At the end of the five days, whether their activities were legal or illegal, cultural, or psychedelic, the soldiers returned to the R & R centers for the trip back to Vietnam. They were always tired and broke, but in most cases, substantially happier.

My own R & R came after seven months in-country. John and I went together and decided on Manila for five major reasons: it was closest; we had both been there before; everyone spoke English; it was cheap; and the women were gorgeous and very friendly. The plane flew into Clarke Air Base, and we rented a driver in a 1957 Chevy, who took us on a most harrowing drive over mountainous roads to the city of Olongapo, near the Subic Bay Naval Base, which was the largest U.S. military installation outside the contiguous U.S.

33. R & R

The Philippines were discovered on March 17, 1521, by Ferdinand Magellan. The archipelago was named after Spain's King Phillip II, and consisted of 7,107 islands. Its population was around one hundred million. It was part of the Spanish Empire for a little over three hundred years, but during the 1898 Treaty of Paris, it was ceded over to the United States for twenty million dollars. The U.S. granted it commonwealth status in 1935. The earliest settlers were of Asian descent, but after the influx of the Spanish, and the commingling of the ethnic groups, the Filipino people are of a Euro-Asian ethnicity. This mixture gives the women a very exotic and beautiful look.

John and I checked into a hotel in downtown Olongapo, secured two rooms, and put all of our money in the hotel safe. We then directed the concierge to supply one bottle of vodka, a few joints, extra towels, and a different woman each day for the next five days for each of us. We left explicit instructions that we were only to be disturbed in case of fire, earthquake, or the eruption of Mt. Pinatubo; and in the case of Mt. Pinatubo, we were only to be notified when the lava flow got closer than five hundred yards.

We left the hotel rooms a couple of times during our stay. Those short forays were for a few outside dining experiences and some walking tours through the town, although Olongapo consisted of five hundred bars and three hundred hotels. What Olongapo lacked in culture and interesting tourist destinations, it more than made up for with a wide variety and an unlimited number of stunningly beautiful women. We had most meals sent up to us and our companions in our rooms. We took our "dates" with us to the restaurants we visited, and they were very appreciative. We even took them shopping in the outdoor mall for some new clothes and shoes.

Of course, after five days of this we were still not ready to go back to Vietnam and the war. But the ramifications for missing one's return flight were severe. You were considered Absent Without Leave (AWOL), and could be arrested and jailed. The kicker was that your jail time would not begin until your tour in Vietnam was over. That was a very good incentive to make your flight back, and complete your tour of duty. John and I reluctantly checked out, gathered up our remaining $22.00 (between us) from the hotel safe, and once again rode over the mountains back to Clarke AFB, and our flight back to Cam Ranh Bay.

R & R made everyone's tour somewhat bearable, as it gave the soldiers something to look forward to, and, in most cases, something to look fondly back on. In regards to the abundance of sexual activities on those trips, it brought to mind Winston Churchill's famous quote about the Royal Air

Force (RAF) in World War II, although using a bit of literary license, in respect to R & R, it could read: "Never before, in the field of human conflict, was so much, done to so many, by so few."

Whoever came up with the concept of R & R probably prevented countless more cases of mental problems popping up among the participants of this specific war. Vietnam, in particular, was very taxing on the psyche of those who participated. Unlike previous wars such as World War I, World War II, and the Korean War, there were no obvious lines where the enemy was on one side, and the "good guys" were on the other. Nor did the enemy wear identifying uniforms. In Vietnam, we didn't even know who the enemy was most of the time, as the Viet Cong were villagers, farmers, and fishermen during the day and soldiers at night. That is the main reason that so many civilians were killed. There was no "their side" or "our side" as far as what geographical areas were inhabited by whom. Anyone could be carrying a bomb. Anyone could be the enemy. Anyone could kill you.

34

BUS RIDES AND OX CARTS

We got up just in time for another fantastic breakfast on the *Angkor*. Our excursion for the day began after we docked in Prek Dam, and then hopped on a bus for the ride to another temple. It was one more magnificent complex housing about seventy Buddhist monks, along with monks in training, and white-robed nuns. I still couldn't get the picture of fighting monks out of my head.

The nuns consisted mostly of elderly women who were disenfranchised in one way or another; the monks took them in and allowed them to live out their remaining years in the temples by doing the cooking. It worked well for all concerned.

We boarded the bus and headed for Kampong Tralech, where we met a number of ox carts. We were assigned two to a cart, and boarded, facing backwards, with the last one hanging his or her legs over the rear of the cart. The ox cart took off. Well, "took off" might be incorrect. "Inched forward" or "barely moved" might be a better description, as ox carts are not a mode of transportation for anyone that might be in a hurry to get anywhere. Little girls on the side of the road, walking, were passing us, and little girls take really little steps.

Each cart was followed by a group of young kids, hoping to get paid for their companionship at the end of the trip. One follower sang for us, and pointed out in English, every noun we encountered along the way. The one bad thing about being the back person in an ox cart is that the following cart has no idea when you are going to slow down or stop. Because there are no brake lights on ox carts, the following oxen, and their wet, disgusting noses, become one with you. This might be due to slow reaction times on the part of the oxen, or the ox-cart driver. Both seemed to have equivalent levels of awareness.

The other noticeable thing is that those people, after countless millennia,

The huge monastery at Prek Dam, Cambodia, where much of the training of new monks takes place. Large and ornate, it covers many acres.

still didn't really have the concept of the wheel down perfectly. The rest of the world took it for granted that the wheel, since its very inception, should be round. "Round" is actually a word used in the definition of a wheel. Unfortunately, those ox-cart wheels were only "almost" round ... and "almost" round did not make for a smooth ride no matter how fast or slow you were moving.

Top: The housing facility at the monastery in Prek Dam where monks and monk trainees sleep and eat their meals. *Bottom:* My wife and I taking an ox cart ride in Kampong Tralech, very possibly the slowest mode of transportation ever conceived by man.

The town barbershop in Kampong Tralech, right on the river ... so you can get a haircut with a nice river view.

We eventually made it to the other end of town in around a half hour (not bad for two blocks), and walked the rest of the way through the town market to our ship, passing many "speeding" ox carts on the way. We also passed the town barbershop, on the bank of the river.

We returned to the *Angkor*, and the rest of the day was spent aboard,

34. Bus Rides and Ox Carts

with no excursions planned for the afternoon. Lunch was served, and once again the choices were all good. Picture a bird's nest–shaped scrambled egg filled with pad thai noodles and shrimp ... absolutely delicious.

One of the creations by the ship's chef consisted of a sort of open omelet in the shape of a nest, filled with pad thai and shrimp. Excellent!

35

On Watch

Meals like bird's-nest shrimp and Pad Thai were not ever available on my previous trip to Vietnam. Especially when I had the mundane job of night security watch in Cam Ranh Bay, sitting in a bunker, with one other sailor, watching the beach through the jungle.

"You know, Vinny, I hate this crap; sitting in this hole for four hours in the middle of the night. It's dark as hell and we can't even see anything. What a waste of time. If the VC wanted to, they could just sneak right by us; and we wouldn't even notice them."

"You're right, Rich, there's a lot of other things I'd rather be doing right now than standing watch. I'd rather be sleeping, for one. Or you know what? I'd rather be getting laid. I haven't gotten laid in so long in this stinking place, I don't even know if it still works any more. Actually, even more than that, I'd sooner be back in the Big Apple right now doing anything. I really miss Laurie. Who knows what she's doing right now, or who she's doing right now. Probably out on a date giving away some of her good stuff."

"Nah, bull, you get a letter from her every day. She wouldn't go out on you. Here, take a hit of this. It's really good stuff. I got it from the old man that does the gardening over by the mess hall. I swear, they got the best grass in the world here in Nam. It's the only thing that makes it almost tolerable. Come on, I got plenty more, it'll make you feel better."

"Rich, did you see that? Someone just ran across the beach up there, just past the jungle line."

"You're full of crap! I didn't see anything. It must be the grass. I told you it was good stuff."

"No, man, I really saw something. Think we ought to check it out?"

"Yeah, sure, Vinny, you go check it out. I'll cover you. I'm not leaving the bunker. It's too dark, and besides, I'm too fucked up."

35. On Watch

"Yeah, maybe you're right, give me another hit. Good thing the lieutenant never comes out here to check on us, but I heard he smokes too. Probably wouldn't hassle us over it, you think?"

"Who gives a damn? No one here really cares what anyone else does, as long as he gets his year done and gets the hell out of here. It's just a matter of rotating bodies, alive or dead, it doesn't matter. Just stay alive for your year, any way you can, and you're out of here. I got seventy one days left, and then it's back to 'the World.' Miami, land of sun, fun and semi-clad beach beauties. Vinny, roll another joint, will ya? Wait a minute, I just saw someone run across the beach up there. At least I think I did. No, hell, I did. Give me the radio. I'm gonna call HQ and report this and see what they want us to do.

"HQ, this is bunker four. Do you read? Over."

"Bunker four, HQ, go ahead. We read you, over."

"Ah, yeah, Dreesen, this is Rich, I think we just saw someone out here on the edge of the woods, running across the beach, over."

"What the hell do you mean, you think you saw someone? Did you, or didn't you? Over."

"Well, actually we both saw something. Ask the lieutenant what we should do, over."

"Rich, this is Lt. Jameson, who are you on watch with? Over."

"Ah, lieutenant, it's Vinny and me, sir. Why? Over."

"Because I know you two guys, and I don't doubt for a second that you could be hallucinating out there, but on the chance you are not, the next time you see someone run across the beach, challenge him, over."

"Aye, aye, sir. Over."

"Damn, Vinny, the lieutenant's known all along about us smoking out here on watch. I guess everyone does it. Don't you think that if they thought it was so bad, they would have stopped it a long time ago?"

"You're right, pass me the joint. Look, there he goes again! Maybe it's a whole platoon of VC landing here. HALT! WHO GOES THERE? STAND AND IDENTIFY YOURSELF! Rich, they didn't stop. What do we do now? Maybe we should just wait a few minutes and see what happens. It really doesn't look like a whole platoon or anything, just maybe one guy lost … trying to get some of our grass. Here's the joint."

"Vinny, you asshole, why would anyone sneak up on us to get our grass in a country where it costs two dollars a pound, grows wild, and can be picked anywhere? Nah, I bet it's a scout, or a saboteur coming in to blow up the base. Is your M-16 loaded? You even remember how it works? You probably haven't fired it in weeks. Funny about this place: we're in the middle of a freaking war zone, but hardly anything ever happens here. Didn't you ever think that was weird? I mean, all around us there's fighting, and when we go out on patrol in the boats, we always get ambushed and shot at and shit, but here at the base, which is pretty exposed, nothing ever happens. Oh yeah, except for that sapper [Viet Cong commandos or special task troops] attack last month. But that was the only attack ever on this base. Pass me the joint. It's almost like we got a deal with the enemy on certain bases. You leave this one of ours alone, and we'll leave that one of yours alone. Pretty God-damned weird if you ask me. Don't you think so, Vinny? Vinny, wake up, you idiot. You know what happens if they catch you sleeping on watch? Even here?"

"What? Oh shit, I must have dozed off. When's that roving patrol going to show up with the coffee and sandwiches? I'm getting hungry. Rich, look, there he goes again! HALT! WHO GOES THERE? STAND AND IDENTIFY YOURSELF … you son of a bitch. Give me that radio.

"HQ, this is bunker four again. Do you read me? Over."

"Bunker four. This is HQ. We read you, go ahead. Over."

"HQ, bunker four, we saw him again, and challenged him, but he didn't respond. It seems to be only one guy, over."

"Bunker four, HQ, we're sending the roving patrol up there to check this out. Keep your weapons at the ready, and keep extra alert, over."

"HQ, bunker four, we read, over."

"Here, Vinny, take the last hit off this, and then stash it somewhere. The rover will be here in four or five minutes, and I don't know who it is tonight. It could be that jerk lifer, O'Neill. I don't trust him as far as I can throw that dumb fuck. I'll never understand why anyone in their right mind would stay in the Navy any longer than he has to. O'Neill has been in for like twelve years now, and he's already an E-5. What a fucking loser. Anyway, make sure the grass is hidden, in case it is him. I don't want to have to put up with any bullshit with only seventy-one days left in country."

"Hey, don't worry, I got enough on O'Neill where he wouldn't say anything, even if he caught us doing his mother. He may be a lifer, and only an E-5 after twelve years, but that doesn't mean he's a total moron. He's into black market greenbacks. His wife sends him real dollars in packages of cookies and shit, and he trades them in in Saigon at about five to one for Piasters, and then trades the P's in for Military Payment Certificates (MPC) here on the base and buys money orders to send back to his wife. He's made about fifty grand in the past eight months."

"What? Are you screwing with me? That stupid jerk figured that out?

Front and back views of the Military Payment Certificates which were used in lieu of American greenbacks in order to keep American currency off the local markets.

Unbelievable. Well, I sure got a lot more respect for him now, anyway. I knew he had to be here for a reason. A guy with twelve years in didn't have to come here at all. Un-fucking-real! Here comes the truck. I hope he brought the coffee and sandwiches, and maybe a few Snickers bars."

"Hey, O'Neill, is that you?"

"Yeah, Vinny, what's up? They say you saw someone up here, on the beach. What's the story? By the way, here's your coffee and sandwiches. Hope you like ham. I forgot the cream, but there's plenty of sugar. Now, where did you see this guy? Or have you guys been smoking some of that shit, and just think you saw someone?"

"No, man, we really saw someone. See, right up there past the tree line on the beach. That's where he was, ran right across there, three times. We challenged him twice but nothing happened."

"Maybe he just doesn't understand English, Vinny."

"Yeah, right, O'Neill. If he doesn't understand English, he shouldn't be where he is."

"OK, look, I got plenty of coffee. The lieutenant told me to stay up here with you guys until we determine what the hell is really going on. Hey, shit, I just saw something. It looked like someone running across the beach. HALT! WHO GOES THERE? STAND AND IDENTIFY YOURSELF. Come on, you son of a bitch, identify yourself. That's it! You guys get your weapons at the ready and put a round in the chamber.

"HQ, O'Neill up at bunker four, come in, over."

"Bunker four, HQ. What is it, O'Neill? Over."

"HQ, bunker four, I saw it. Whatever it was that they saw, I saw it too. We are cocked and loaded. Should we open fire next time? We have challenged three times now with no response. Over."

"Bunker four, HQ, the lieutenant says for you to report back here and let the two watches take care of it. They have permission to shoot. They are to stay in contact and keep us apprised of the situation, over."

"HQ, bunker four, we read loud and clear. I'm on my way, over. See you two guys later. You heard what they said, keep in contact. There's only about 45 minutes left until light. Maybe nothing will happen. Later."

"Rich, what the hell is going on here? They know there is something up here. Why don't they send some more guys up here?"

"Hey, our watch is up in like forty-five minutes. Maybe nothing will happen, like O'Neill said. And, besides, it's only one guy that we saw."

"I don't know, Rich. I'm scared shitless. There he is again. I'm firing. You shoot too, I don't want to miss."

"Shit, you think we got him? I fired my whole fucking magazine. What about you, Vin, how many rounds you get off? We must have hit him, you hear that scream?"

"Damn, I fired my whole magazine too. That's sixty rounds between us, we must have hit him. I heard the scream too. You want to go check it out?"

35. On Watch

"Hell no, Vinny, let's wait until there's some light. It's only a few more minutes. I'm not going out into the jungle in the dark. Hurry, light another joint, my heart is beating like a jackhammer. I can't stop shaking. I never been this close to anyone that I killed. It was always out in the boat, shooting into the jungle, never having to see it. I don't like this. I'm glad I'm not in the Army. Those guys have to do this shit all the time."

"HQ, bunker four, do you read? Over."

"Bunker four, HQ, we read. Over."

"HQ, bunker four, we fired at the intruder and think we got him. We will check it out as soon as it gets a little lighter. There is no more movement on the beach, over."

"Bunker four, HQ, we read. Your reliefs will be there soon. Check out the situation, and report back to us on your way off watch. Over."

"Rich, it's getting light, let's go check it out before our reliefs get here. It's been real quiet out there since the shooting."

"Sure, Vin, I'll go check it out."

"OK, I'll cover you, but be careful, it could be a trap. Can't trust these guys, you know. I mean, they are the enemy, right? Just be careful."

"Jesus Christ, Vinny, come here, you gotta see this. It's a fucking tiger, man. I don't believe it, a goddamned tiger. We must have hit it forty times."

"Oh, man, Rich, unreal. You want the skin?"

"What? Look at it, it's full of holes and blood. What kind of place is this? Why am I here? In my whole life I never thought I'd be in the same place as a tiger. Come on, let's get out of here, here come our watch reliefs."

"Richie, Vinny, what's happening? How was your watch? Anything exciting happening, or just the usual shit? You know, trying to stay awake, a lot of nothing to see and lot of nothing to do."

"Yeah, yeah, sure, guys. Look, have a good watch and keep alert."

"Sure, Richie, go catch some sleep. By the way, got any grass?"

36

Busses, Goat Roads and Angkor Thom

The topography changed as the *Angkor* steamed north, with far less vegetation, sparser tree growth, and very little river traffic. There were mountains in the distance on both sides of the Ton Le Sap. It looked like a savannah, flat land for miles until the mountains began. It was beautifully verdant, the weather bearable, and the humidity was not overwhelming. A slight breeze blew as the ship steamed north to the mouth of Ton Le Sap Lake.

We were informed that we would not be able to traverse the lake to our destination of Siem Reap because the water level was far too low for the ship to manage. This level changed with each cruise. Sometimes the ship entered Ton Le Sap Lake and steamed all the way to Siem Reap.

That piece of the river, just south of the lake, was a very beautiful, peaceful stretch with small villages sporadically placed along the shore on both sides. An occasional boat passed us, and children waved and screamed from the shore as we passed slowly by. There were families and groups of river nomads. Those were people who moved up and down the rivers in their sampans, toting all that they owned, and making camp wherever they decided to stop, usually for a week or less at each location. They stayed at each place for up to a week at a time, but usually for a shorter length. During that time they set up temporary encampments, and then fished, and hunted small animals. It was a very simple but labor-intensive way of life. They lived without any of the modern conveniences that we take for granted. No electricity, no refrigeration, no ice … just the barest of necessities to sustain daily life. They were this part of the world's equivalent to desert nomads.

The passengers were resting, or reading, or discussing a host of subjects

36. Busses, Goat Roads and Angkor Thom

Floating homes, a flat savannah, and distant mountains as seen from the deck of the *Angkor* as we cruised northward.

with each other. It was just a time of reflection and inner peace, with a lot of quiet solitude going on as the river, and its sights, glided slowly by. There was no movie tonight and most of the passengers crashed after the evening meal.

The next morning we were all up early for our last wake-up on the ship. Everyone was packed, and on their way to our final ship's meal. The crew loaded the entirety of our luggage onto a truck, and we were promised that it would be at the hotel in Siem Reap when we arrived. We grabbed our numerous carry-on bags, headed for our very luxurious, upscale bus, and prepared for the upcoming five-hour bus ride to Siem Reap.

River nomads along the Mekong. They travel together and live together in their temporary stops up and down the river and its tributaries. This is a never-ending life-long journey for most of them.

The ride started, and we were warned about the first 15–20 kilometers, which was called the "Goat Road," ostensibly because goats traveled on it, or once traveled on it. I believe it was so named because the road was actually built by goats. That's what it felt like. A top speed of maybe 30 kph (about 18 mph) was attained for this part of the trip. Fortunately,

36. Busses, Goat Roads and Angkor Thom

the Chinese have invested money to improve the road. We came upon construction crews, which eerily resembled many of the Department of Transportation (DOT) crews in the States. You know, the ones with nine men standing around watching, while one guy pats down the road with a shovel. Some things never changed, no matter where you went in the world. We eventually left the goat road, and hit a nice paved road.

In another forty minutes or so we stopped for a "happy house" (bathroom) break at a combination outdoor restaurant, market, and potato chip shop. Some of the delicacies that were available included deep fried tarantulas, which seemed to be a local favorite, and fried cockroaches. I tried neither. Also available were short pieces of bamboo stuffed with sticky rice and beans. There were a plethora of potato chips on the shelves in such flavors as sushi, kim-chee, New York steak, jalapeño, and my personal favorite, seaweed. Nothing says, "I bet you can't eat just one," like a seaweed-flavored potato chip.

At a rest stop along the highway to Angkor Wat, many types of foodstuffs were being sold to both tourists and locals ... like deep-fried tarantulas. Not my thing, but they make a nice photograph.

The twelve-hundred-year-old temple at Angkor Thom, just outside the city of Siem Reap, built by the Buddhist King Jayavarman VII.

After the break, we were back on the road again, as we passed kilometer after kilometer of rice paddies, lily ponds, and a multitude of other crop plots. Eventually, we reached Siem Reap, a bustling tourist-filled shopping mecca with lots of beautiful buildings, gorgeous hotels, museums, markets, and thousands of small businesses. We headed straight for the ruins of Angkor Thom, over a thousand years old, built by the Buddhist King Jayavarman VII. There were hundreds of busses and thousands of tourists there.

Our new tour guide, Tek, was quite informative. But I just don't get it. A thousand years ago, Buddhists and Hindi happened upon this somewhat idyllic spot that even then was quite in the middle of nowhere. They spent hundreds of years building all these structures with multi-ton rocks that they had to ferry up the river from over 50 kilometers away. Each rock was cut to fit perfectly to the next, and the intricate reliefs were carved into each of the stones with primitive tools. Such labor-intensive work took decades upon decades to accomplish by thousands and thousands of artisans and slaves. So I figured either these people had nothing else to do, or they created busy work so that everyone had a job. They could, much more easily, have built log cabins for everyone in about six or eight weeks, thrown in a few totem poles to honor their numerous gods, and lived a very complacent, easy life. I mean, this is a jungle with

36. Busses, Goat Roads and Angkor Thom

forests full of trees and lumber available nearby. I think that Native Americans had the right idea. But, if that were the case here, no one would be visiting Siem Reap and it would be just another little sleepy backwater town in the wilds of Cambodia right at the end of the Ton Le Sap River. I guess there is a reason for everything.

37

LIFE ON THE RIVER AND GETTING SHOT

This trip, so far, has shown just how dependent the people who live on the Mekong and connecting rivers were on those bodies of water for their very existence. Be it fishing, farming, transportation, power, or even a home ... it all goes back to the Mekong, and its hundreds of tributaries, to supply those necessities of life to millions. It brings and supports life to everyone on it in one way or another. My previous trips on the rivers, decades ago, did not teach me that. The rivers then were deadly, and seemed sometimes to even be evil and foreboding, full of ambushes, mines, and other boats loaded with who knows what. At night there were noises, shadows, and glimpses of things not quite clear enough to make out. It was chilling. During daylight hours, when we did 99 percent of our traveling and patrolling, our awareness had to be exemplary.

You never knew what you were going to see or witness as you made even one more turn in the river. You might even stumble upon a helicopter landing on a small river patrol boat. Or you might have your boat passed by a speeding Patrol Air Cushioned Vehicle (PACV) gliding across the surface like an Everglades airboat, as you cruised up or down the river. We had to watch closely all the time as we wended our way along the rivers or the next thing we might encounter could be death.

My first confrontation with death was a bloated, black body, floating in the river. Floaters always turned black. We smelled it first, a smell you don't soon forget. Then we saw it. It looked similar to a manatee. It was swollen, semi-submerged, and dark. We kept going; we were a bit more somber, but we kept going. Floating bodies became almost commonplace after a while and, but for the smell, we hardly noticed... almost. How sad that the stench of death should become the norm.

37. Life on the River and Getting Shot

My LCM-8 boat in the foreground, being passed by a Patrol Air Cushioned Vehicle (PACV). It skimmed across the water on an inflated bag of air, propelled by a rear engine, with an aircraft propeller attached, much like an Everglades air boat.

Neither I nor any of my crew members ever indiscriminately killed anyone else. On some of the boats, it was a sport, shooting people as you traveled up the river, just because they were there ... and just because you could. My crew and I had a very curious and serious conversation about this. We tried to figure out how we could best control our behavior and maintain some semblance of civility amid the barbarity that surrounded us. We had no rules, no limitations, nothing to guide us. This was a circumstance that was encountered by very few people during their lifetimes. We could do whatever we wanted to anyone we wanted in our travels. A good number of others took advantage of that situation. There would be no repercussions for outright murder, or rape, or robbing the indigenous people of their meager belongings. We talked it over and, after much discussion, decided that the best way to control our behavior was that we would vow never to do anything we could not tell our mothers about. It

As amazing as it may seem, helicopters were oftentimes able to land on 49′ long Tango boats for various reasons: deliver ammo, pick up wounded, deliver supplies. It was a very precarious job for the chopper pilots.

seemed to be a simple solution to a mind-boggling problem, but it worked. We were as civil as the situation would allow.

The strangest occurrence happened one day as we were cruising the Vam Co Dong. My previous engineman and R & R buddy, John from Chicago, had been transferred out, and was replaced by John from Texas, an easygoing, amiable guy. He was tall and slender, with sandy blond hair and a broad happy face. He was a very good mechanic and kept our engines in top shape. As we traveled the river, we watched the banks and the jungle for anything out of the ordinary. We strained our eyes watching, hoping to see nothing. Usually hours passed with nothing happening at all, sometimes days, then all of a sudden, a firefight.

We were ambushed. One side of the river broke out in bullets and rockets. Once again, rounds pinged against the metal plate around the pilot house, as my crew jumped into action. The noise was deafening. The adrenaline was flowing. Screams were heard. Dennis and Dale, on the .50 and the M-60, were firing back into the jungle. John grabbed his M-16, and as I always did under this circumstance, I put the engines in all-ahead-full and immediately picked up the radio and called in air support.

It was a habit of mine to stay very cognizant of exactly where we were

37. Life on the River and Getting Shot

on the river at any given point in time. I was obsessive about following the charts as we moved along. I knew exactly where we were all the time, and where to send the air support.

As we got out of firing range, and I fired the last round from my M-79 grenade launcher into the jungle, I looked on the deck in front of the wheelhouse and saw John lying there, in a growing pool of blood. There was blood everywhere. He wasn't wearing a shirt and I saw a huge hole in his back. I put Dale on the wheel of the boat and went to see if there was anything I could do for John.

At this point it turned into the scene from every war movie

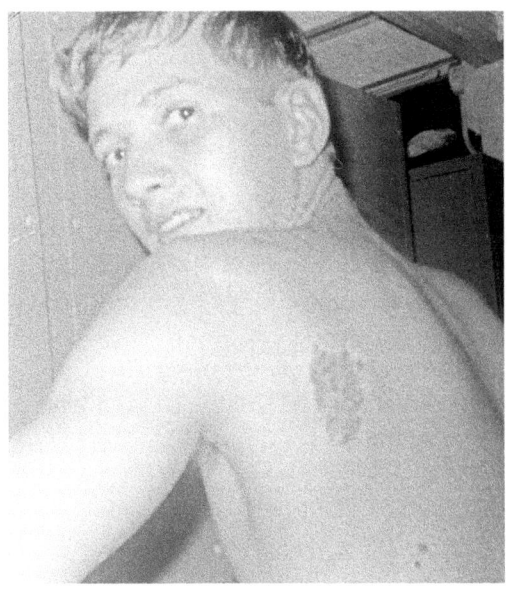

My crewmate John, from Texas, showing off his cleaned-up back wound, after being ambushed on the river.

I had ever watched. I squatted down on the deck and took John into my arms, his head resting in the crook of my elbow ... his blood dripping, covering me. I was lost. I thought he was dead. I wasn't sure as to what to do. Death hadn't been quite this close before, or this personal. It had always been out in the jungle, unseen, or floating in the river, face down.

Then, his eyes opened slowly and he looked up and focused on me. Softly and slowly he said, "Rich, do me a favor." I thought to myself, *Oh shit, here it comes*. I was waiting for the "Tell my mother I love her, or tell my girl she was the only one," or some such trite movie quote. I waited for it, my emotions building, getting myself ready to comfort him, and holding back my own tears. Then he said softly, "Do you have a camera?" You know that famous incredulous crooked sneer that Clint Eastwood uses in almost all of his movies when he hears or sees something utterly inane? Well, that crossed my face as I thought, and almost yelled, *WHAT? A camera? What the fuck are you talking about?* He then sat up with his back to me, and his head turned over his shoulder looking at me, and said, "Yeah, yeah, can you get a picture of this?" It seems that the bullet had hit him parallel to his back, taking out a shallow chunk of skin, as opposed to striking him perpendicular to his body and entering him. It is what is commonly referred to as a "flesh wound," but the chunk of skin was about as big as a small tortilla, and there was blood everywhere. I dropped him out of my lap and got him his camera, as I thought to myself, *That son of a bitch!* and took some pics for him. I then cleaned him up and took another picture with my own camera. I can say proudly and with full truthfulness that no one on any of the numerous boats I captained was killed. Some of us were wounded, yes; injured, yes; but no deaths.

I called for a med-evac chopper to lift John off for treatment. They showed up in about 20 minutes, loaded him from the place we had pulled into on the side of the river, and we never saw him again. I was freaked out for a good hour, and pulled into an ATSB for some rest and food, then headed back to Nha Be to get a new engineman. This place just kept wigging me out.

38

THE HOTEL AND NEW YEAR'S EVE

We finally got to the hotel in Siem Reap, and it was gorgeous. The lobby was full of plants and ornately decorated tile floors and walls. We checked in and got our keys, once again hassle-free, due to the incredible organizational skills of our tour director, Mark Nichols. The room was beautifully appointed, with fresh flowers, and bright printed draperies and bedspreads. The view from the balcony was dazzling, as the U-shaped hotel encompassed a pool and patio area surrounded by lush, tropical vegetation. Waterfalls and bamboo pole umbrellas added to the jungle-like atmosphere. The Victoria Angkor Resort was five-star all the way. We took much-needed showers and a little relaxation before meeting Steve and Debbie down in the lobby at 7:45.

A month before the trip, I perused the Internet for a place to have New Year's Eve dinner. The cruise directors informed us that New Year's Eve would be the only dinner that we would be on our own. I knew we would be there in Siem Reap, and chose the Touiche Restaurant after conversing by e-mail with the owner. He reserved a table for us and told us he would send someone to our hotel to pick us up in a tuk-tuk. Right on time, the tuk-tuk driver sent by the restaurant showed up and took us for a ride into what we originally thought must have been the human trafficking part of the city. It was a dark, bumpy, seedy-looking part of town. We thought for sure that we were well on our way into the clutches of white slavers, or some other such dastardly situation.

And then, like an oasis in the desert, a beautifully appointed, brightly lit little restaurant appeared before us. We went in and saw a "Reserved" sign on our table, and were seated by a pleasant and attractive Cambodian girl. She took our drink order, then our food order. Mary and Debbie

The lush pool and patio area of the Victoria Angkor Resort Hotel in Siem Reap, surrounded by waterfalls and tropical vegetation.

ordered the snapper, and Steve and I ordered the Australian T-bone steaks. The fish presentation was impressive; a banana leaf–wrapped whole snapper for each of our wives, which was expertly unwrapped, skinned, and filleted by the young waitress. It was absolutely beautiful and delicious. The steaks were cooked to perfection and minimally spiced. The white wine choice, which we left up to our waitress was excellent, according to the girls, and complemented their fish perfectly. The beer was served ice cold, exactly how Steve and I ordered it. The side dishes of assorted local vegetables and potatoes were well chosen, and well cooked by the chefs. For dessert, we shared coconut custard and kuay namuan, which is a traditional Cambodian dessert consisting of bananas cooked in coconut milk. Both were tasty and a nice sweet ending to the meal. That entire magnificent meal came to $84.00 for the four of us, including tip. All was well in the world. After dinner, we decided to head back to the hotel, opting out of the pre-planned shopping trip tonight, because we were very tired after the tedious bus ride and the day of sightseeing at the ruins. The hotel New Year's party went on loudly until around 2:30 a.m., and an end came to a very long, very interesting day.

39

CAM RANH BAY

New Year's of 1970 was a bit different. I spent it in Cam Ranh Bay, Vietnam, at the Naval Repair Facility (NRF). Cam Ranh was considered to be the premier deep-water shelter in all of Southeast Asia. NRF was located at the southern tip of a long peninsula, right at the entrance to the huge bay, known in Vietnamese as *Mui Cha Da*. Being at the tip of a peninsula, it fronted both the bay and the South China Sea. The main buildings, repair shops, and piers were on the eastern bay side, while the South China Sea or western side of the peninsula, had a lush, sandy, curved beach. The Navy's Special Services office supplied surfboards and small sailboats to anyone who wanted them.

NSF was home to Coastal Division 14, made up of anywhere from ten to fifteen 50' Swift Boats, and later became the administrative center for Operation Market Time. The waters around the base, including the central coast areas of Vietnam, were home to several of the Market Time Swift Boat Groups. Operation Market Time was the Navy's effort to halt the flow of troops and supplies from North Vietnam into South Vietnam from the sea. The Swift Boats normally operated from the coast to two miles out.

NRF Cam Ranh was small (400 men) and somewhat isolated from the huge Army and Air Force installations on the northern side of the peninsula. Due to the presence of those two large bases, NSF was relatively secure, seeing very little actual combat action in and around the base. Its main function was repairing and refitting all battle-damaged boats. They could actually build an entirely new boat in the various shops around the base. There were welding shops, woodworking shops, boiler shops, engine repair shops, and weapon refurbishing shops. There was a huge corrugated steel hut where boats could be sandblasted and repainted, and one submersible dry-dock for lifting boats out of the water for an assortment of repairs that could not be accomplished while the boat was afloat.

There was also a signpost with mileages to various cities, both in the U.S. and elsewhere. It reminded us of how far from reality, and the real world, we really were; Washington, D.C., 10,415 miles; Dallas, 9,012 miles; Paris, 4,801 miles; London, 4,987 miles; and numerous other locations around the world.

According to the Navy, and the people who didn't actually have to participate in a war, one of the advantages to being in a war zone was that you didn't have to pay postage when mailing a letter back to the States, which I guess made being in life-threatening positions on a daily basis all worth it. I mean, all I had to do to save the twelve-cent postage on letters home was to put my life in danger and possibly shoot and kill other people. What a deal!

My job in Cam Ranh was threefold. I was one of two base divers, doing all sorts of repair and recovery diving, recovering anything from dropped tools and jewelry to engine parts, and repairing the underside of some of the boats. I was a certified Navy Diver, having gone to Dive School. I replaced damaged propellers and rudders. I also set up an underwater lighting system around the dock area that helped to prevent enemy swimmers from sneaking up on the base at night. The lights allowed the watch personnel to spot any waterborne intrusions into the dock area. That lighting system was installed with the assistance of civilian representatives from the company that designed and manufactured the system. The light

An example of the envelopes supplied by the military for use by those in a war zone. No postage was necessary to mail those letters.

bulbs used were approximately the size of your thumb, and they were encased in a waterproof glass tube which was secured to the base into which the bulb was attached. Each bulb unit was attached to the next by insulated wiring. The bulbs produced so much heat, each being five hundred watts, in such a small area, that the installer could not touch the bulbs with his fingers, lest his skin oil get on the glass, causing the bulb to explode when turned on. No foreign objects other than the foam that they were shipped in could touch the bulbs. The chart of where the system was to be installed was studied intensely before installation, as the grid was predetermined in order to give the most coverage with the smallest number of lights.

In addition to those dive jobs, I also had the difficult and depressing job of recovering bodies, either from downed aircraft or from sunken boats. Every dive I made had to be followed up by filling out the front and back side of a dive form explaining every facet of each dive: diver name, location of dive, date, depth, wave height, current, water temperature, water visibility, bottom time, number of dives in the previous twenty-four hours, and on the back, the description of the dive, and outcome. I saved most of those forms.

Having a diver present had some advantages for the rest of the sailors of NRF. About once a week, Reilly (the other diver) and I would take a couple of mesh bags with us for dives out in the bay. We would retrieve lobsters, many lobsters. These were similar to Florida lobster, which lacked claws, but had plenty of delicious meat in the tails and legs. For some reason that I cannot understand, the locals never fished for lobster. They were plentiful, large and easy to get with our homemade three-pronged spears. We could bring up over a hundred lobsters in a little over an hour. We just loaded the mesh bags, brought them back to the awaiting rope below the boat, and our topside tender would hoist it up, empty it into a container, and send the bag back down for another refill. Once back at the dock area, the lobsters were taken to the mess hall, and the cooks would do their magic.

Upon occasion, we were called upon to create goodwill with the people who lived in the villages surrounding the bay area. We would periodically pick up a number of locals in my LCM-6 boat and take them out to the small cove in Binh Ba Island, at the entrance to Cam Ranh Bay. Once there, my crew would secure the anchor and we would then toss a few concussion grenades into the water near the boat. A couple of minutes later, stunned fish would float to the surface and the village children would jump into the water and retrieve them, tossing them up to eagerly awaiting

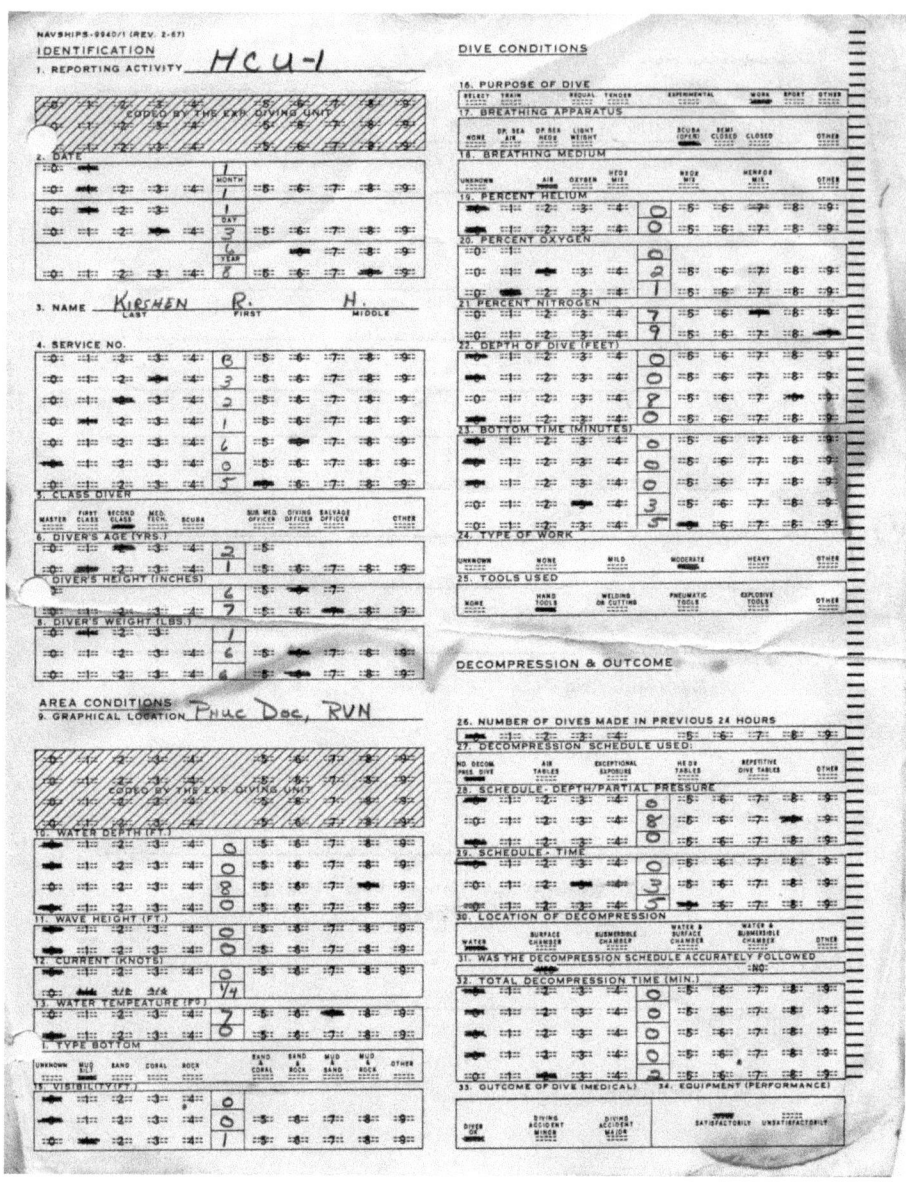

The front side of a Navy Dive report, which had to be completed after every dive made by a U.S. Navy Diver.

hands. We could usually obtain enough fish, using that explosive method of fishing, to feed the entire village for a day or two, with much less effort than they would have spent catching that amount of fish the traditional way.

My other responsibility was driving the boat that ferried the nonmil-

35. DECOMPRESSION STOPS

DEPTH	TIME	GAS
NONE		

36. JOB DESCRIPTION

RECOVERY OF U.S. AIR FORCE PILOT'S BODY.

37. ADDITIONAL REMARKS

MARINE GROWTH ON BODY AND PARTS OF BODY EATEN BY CRABS.

38. SIGNATURES

DIVING SUPERVISOR	DIVING OFFICER

The reverse side of the same dive sheet, showing the reason for the dive, the results of the dive, and any other comments by the diver.

itary employees back and forth each day from their village, across the bay, to the base, and back again after work hours. Those daily trips afforded me the opportunity to meet and get to know some of the locals. I became friendly with many of the young ladies who worked in various jobs around the base, and some of the men who were the gardeners and painters.

Being captain of one of only two boats that was assigned to the repair facility, and not part of any of the patrol squadrons, made me a good friend to have for many of the men stationed there. As I stated, the base was isolated at the tip of a peninsula. There was no village or city near the base. The closest village was the one across the bay where I transported the workers to and from each day. That was the closest place that anyone on the base could hope to get any female companionship, and I operated the only transportation that could get them there and back. It could have been quite an entrepreneurial undertaking on my part, but that just didn't seem right. The men on the base were very nice to me and my crew of one. We always got to share in everyone's "goody" packages from home, which usually consisted of homemade cookies, candies, or hard-to-come-by canned foods and other specialty items.

On Friday afternoons, when I was making the run across the bay with the base workers, there were invariably six or seven guys wanting a ride to the village for some sexual relief. Those were the guys who did not have the duty over the weekend, and knew that we would pick them up early Monday morning, so that they would be back in time for morning muster. I ran that boat every other week, with another crew operating it on my off week.

One day, one of the Vietnamese men who traveled on my boat daily invited me and my engineman, Jack, to his house in the village for dinner. He said that he would allow us to spend the night there, as he knew we could not get a ride back until the next morning. It was our off-week, so it was possible that we could ride with the other crew on the afternoon run, and return the next morning with them. Jack and I talked it over, and decided we would do it, even though there were rumors that the village was home to a number of Viet Cong sympathizers. Of course, we would be armed.

We rode over with the afternoon boat and followed the man through the village to his house. His house was a small three-room thatch-roofed hut. There was no electricity or running water. There was a community well in the center of the village for water. Light inside the huts was supplied by liquid-fueled flame lanterns attached to the walls. We arrived at his hut, and he introduced us to his wife, who, like himself, spoke little English. We sat on his makeshift porch as his wife disappeared into the village. He lit up a pipe full of marijuana and passed it to us. In a short time, his wife reappeared with a white goose under her arm. The man looked at the goose, then at us and said, "Number one sop sop." We knew that "number one" meant that it was the best. In Vietnam, number one was good, and number ten was bad, no matter what you were referring to: food, drink, a woman, anything. There were no numbers between one and ten, just good or bad. We also knew that "sop-sop" meant food. Then, without any warning the wife took the goose by the head, and spun it around, instantly breaking its neck, right in front of us. She sat down and plucked it, and after plucking, went around to the back of the hut to cook the goose.

In the meantime, the man invited us inside and we sat around a small table. He pulled out three tiny shot glasses, and a corked bottle of clear liquid. He poured three shots and held up his glass and drank it in one swallow. I wasn't much of a drinker, but Jack was. Jack took his in one swallow and his eyes teared and almost popped out of his head as the liquid went down. I took one small sip of mine, but could drink no more of it. As we sat there, Jack pulled out a pack of cigarettes and went to light up, but the man reached across the table and stopped him from lighting his Zippo lighter by grabbing his arm. Jack looked at him questioningly. The man pointed to the burning lanterns on the wall, then to the bottle on the table and said, "No do, same same." Whatever was in the bottle we were drinking from was also lighting the hut, and the man didn't want Jack's mouth to catch on fire.

The wife then came in with a cooked goose, and some green mystery vegetables. We ate it with them, and it was palatable. After dinner he took us for a walk through the village, and we then returned to his hut for another smoke. We were tired now, as were our host and hostess, so they showed us to one of the rooms. It had two straw-type mattresses inside wooden frames, about three feet off the floor.

Jack and I got into the two beds to get some sleep, but in about 15 minutes the man entered the room with two females. They each got into a bed with Jack and me. The man said, *"Mot mon qua cho ban be cua toi"* (a gift for my friends) and left the room. It didn't take Jack and me very long to realize that these were young women ... very young women. They were girls, no more than maybe twelve or thirteen; maybe even younger. We weren't sure as to how to handle this without offending our host. You were not supposed to reject "gifts" from the locals, according to the orientation classes we all took before coming to Vietnam. But this was not our thing. We didn't want any part of it. How would I ever be able to tell my mother about it? We both got out of our beds, and Jack, who spoke a little more Vietnamese than I did, quietly told the girls, *"Khong noi cho an ta"* (don't tell him). They nodded their heads in understanding. Jack and I slept on the floor of the hut, leaving the beds to the two girls. I wasn't sure if it was a normal thing to make an offer like our host did, or if his impression of Americans was so low that he thought it was the norm for us.

Early the next morning, we left the room and thanked our host for his hospitality and his thoughtful gift. He walked us back to the pier area where we boarded the boat for our ride back to the base.

40

ANGKOR WAT AND THE CITADEL OF WOMEN

Mary and I were up at 6:00 a.m. today, after a fantastic sleep in the hotel bed, and enjoyed the more than ample buffet breakfast. Everything you could imagine and once again, many things you could not, was available. Included were eggs, waffles, baguettes, fruit, fried chicken, muesli, pasta, fried sandwiches, and a host of sweets. After eating, we got ready for the trip to Angkor Wat, the largest of the ruins. Aboard the bus, our guide, Tec, told us about Angkor Wat, the most famous of all the Cambodian temples. The massive three-tiered building contained five towers rising almost 200 feet from the ground. It was built by and for King Suryavarman II in the early twelfth century, and dedicated to the Hindu god Vishnu. The enclosed area was 4000' × 5000', almost one square mile. Every wall was covered with hand-chiseled intricate relief work of extraordinary artistic talent, all finely detailed and still clearly legible, after nine centuries in the jungle.

Angkor Wat was taken over by the Buddhists in the 14th century, when, and this is purely conjecture on my part, the Buddhists surmised that it would be far less laborious to take over an existing temple by force, than to build one themselves, which could take a hundred years or so and require feeding and housing thousands of slaves. Good move by the Buddhists, as this particular temple came equipped with a moat, a surrounding protective wall, thousands of beautiful hand carvings, and a multitude of slaves to be used as needed. Those specific amenities were not available in all temples, so the Buddhists made quite the coup there.

From Angkor Wat we headed over to Banteay Srey Temple, which loosely translated was "Citadel of the Women." Not that the temple was built in honor of women, because as we are well aware, most religions of

The famous temples at Angkor Wat, from the 12th century, dedicated to the Hindu god Vishnu. The most famous, and largest, of the Cambodian temples.

40. Angkor Wat and the Citadel of Women

Bantey Srea Temple, or the Citadel of the Women as it was called, due to the beauty of the carvings in the stone.

the world, even to this day, do not honor women very highly or treat them with a great deal of respect. It was more likely because of the delicate beauty of the carvings in the stone that made up the temple. Instead of thinking that maybe some of the men carvers were of the, shall we say, feminine side of life, the Hindus who built it just proclaimed that it was so beautiful, maybe women could have done it. That is, if they had been allowed to do anything other than cook or bear young. It took the reigns of two kings, Rajendravarman and Jayavarman V, to complete the temple, although it was much smaller than most of the other temples constructed in this area. They must not have been very motivated after they realized that some men with varying feminine qualities were doing most of the work. Either that or they used union labor.

On the way through the temple, I was almost prematurely kicked out, but one of the monks was in a forgiving mood, and even smiled as he saw me posing with one of the ancient statues.

Just one more of the incredibly nice people I had met on this trip.

This is me meeting my new best friend at one of he monasteries, to which even the monk who watched me pose cracked a smile.

41

Bare Sole

During the Vietnam War, not everyone I met was as nice and amiable as those I met there as a tourist. Nguyen Cao Thieu (Nu-wen Cow Too) was a wiry, slightly built man who could have weighed no more than forty-five kilos (about a hundred pounds). That in itself was not unusual, as most Vietnamese were notably small in stature. What was unusual about Nguyen was that, in spite of his diminutive proportions, he had the reputation of being tough, and absolutely fearless in combat situations. He was well respected, not only by other Vietnamese soldiers, but also by battle-hardened Americans. American GIs normally had no use or respect for the members of the South Vietnamese military. They didn't consider them to be viable or committed combatants.

I was introduced to Nguyen just prior to leaving Nha Be on one of my many trips up the Vam Co Tay River. He was assigned to my boat as an observer during the Accelerated Turn Over to the Vietnamese (ACTOV) program. This program was instituted to reduce the U.S. troop count in-country, and turn more of the fighting over to the South Vietnamese military forces. He was cordial enough, but even though he was proficient in English, he rarely talked, and usually stayed to himself. He always had this strange cold look in his eyes. It was a look that I had seen before, although not in a Vietnamese, but rather in Americans who enjoyed combat and killing. It was a high to some, as addictive as heroin, and just as deadly.

Six hours north of Nha Be we had our first encounter with the enemy. It appeared to be a loose band of Viet Cong stragglers who had set up an ambush. We really couldn't tell, though, because as usual, when we were ambushed on the river, the attackers were always well hidden in the jungle that grew incessantly along the banks. As soon as the shooting started, I did what we always did when ambushed: I reached for the radio and called for air support. The second thing was to put the boat in all-ahead-full mode and continue up river, out of firing range. There really was no future in staying and fighting because you never knew the strength of the enemy or what weapons they had at their disposal. A look of pure disdain crossed the face of Nguyen as he looked at me, and then a few minutes later at the Huey choppers were lighting up the jungle with their rockets. They were firing into the area which we had just vacated.

As you will recall from an earlier chapter, one of the basic orders we operated under in our river patrol units was that we were never to leave the boat. Chasing enemy troops into the jungle was strictly *verboten*. This rule suited me just fine, as the jungle was plenty scary enough just riding through it on the river. I didn't have to venture into it to test my own machismo.

After spending the night at one of the ATSBs and heading up river in the morning, we again became the object of someone's ire. This time it appeared to be a single sniper, hiding somewhere in the trees, taking potshots at us as we rode by. This was not only life-threatening and annoying, but it also ruined a perfectly good lunch of engine manifold–heated ham and lima beans. As I reached for the radio to call in air support, which one might consider a bit of overkill for one sniper, but the safe thing to do nevertheless, a scrawny little arm with the gripping power of a pit bull grabbed my hand and pulled it away from the handset. As I turned to look, already knowing who I was going to see, my eyes met the cold, penetrating gaze of Nguyen. He lessened the pressure on my hand and asked me if I would consider bringing my boat into the bank of the river and giving him ten minutes to find the sniper. He assured me that if he couldn't find him in the allotted time, we would be on our way, and I could call in the Hueys. I stared into his eyes for a full thirty seconds, while thinking about it, and knew that this was something he had to do.

My crew were already at general quarters, manning their weapons, as was the case whenever we began to take enemy fire. As I pulled the boat into the river bank, to the absolute astonishment of the rest of my crew, Nguyen was off the boat and into the jungle, like a lion leaping off a rock after an unwitting wildebeest. Noiselessly, he left the boat and glided stealthily into the jungle. To this day, I don't know why, but I grabbed my M-16 and some rope, and followed him. I had only left the boat once before, and that was months ago. I never did it again, but this time, I had to see Nguyen at work. I followed as best as I could. Fortunately, I didn't have to go far.

Less than three minutes into the tightly packed jungle I found Nguyen, holding his M-16 to the head of his captive. How he found this guy and captured him so quickly, I will never figure out. Nevertheless,

41. Bare Sole

there we were: Nguyen, the guy in the black pajamas down on his knees, his hands on his head with his fingers interlaced, and me, standing there agape, unable to say or do anything. I became an uninvolved observer. I had rarely been this close to the enemy before, as almost all of our contact had been through the jungle, not eye to eye.

I wasn't sure what to do. I was mesmerized, once again, by this tableau unfolding in front of me. I thought for sure that we would just tie up our captive, bring him back to the boat, and turn him over to the authorities at the next village. They just stared at each other, with obvious loathing. I was frozen. Time had come to a standstill. Sweat dripped down my face. As I watched, Nguyen bent over and removed one of his shoes. He then lifted up his now bare foot and pointed it at the Viet Cong's face about five inches in front of his eyes, still keeping his rifle trained on his captive. He stood in this position for about fifteen or twenty seconds and the prisoner's eyes squinted with hatred, his lips taut. Nguyen put his foot back in his shoe and braced himself. He put the barrel of his M-16 against the Viet Cong's head, and to my utter astonishment, pulled the trigger. I staggered backwards, shocked and shaken. I felt ill as the man's head disappeared in an explosion of bone and brains. It took a minute or two for me to regain what composure I could muster up, my eyes still wide, mouth still open, and heart pounding like a jackhammer. I looked at Nguyen and he looked at me, but no words passed between us. I tried to say something, but no sounds escaped me. We walked back to the boat, boarded, and continued up river without a word between us. It became just one more of those visions that has remained with me and haunted me to this day.

It was six more days before we got back to Nha Be. I still didn't understand the significance of the bare foot, and none of the Americans I asked could shed any light on the meaning of this. The second day back in Nha Be, my crew and I were sitting in the Enlisted Men's Club, throwing back a few brews. Tuy, our waiter, who spoke English, was setting down another round when I explained to him what had occurred back in the jungle with Nguyen. He then enlightened us to the fact that in the Vietnamese culture, the pointing of the bottom of one's bare foot at another person is the single most obscene gesture one imaginable. It is akin to taking all the dirt of the day and rubbing it in someone's face; putting him down and showing utter disdain for him; casting aspersions upon his mother's reputation; and questioning his actual family lineage ... all rolled up into one rather simple gesture.

I can't say that I was much surprised by Tuy's explanation. After the rather ghastly scene that had followed Nguyen's foot gesture, I had somewhat surmised that he wasn't wishing his captive well in the future.

42

HANGING OUT IN TOWN

We headed back to the hotel after visiting the temples, and after about an hour's rest, Steve, Debbie, Mary, and I took a tuk-tuk ride downtown to Pub Street. We had lunch at the Red Piano, made famous in the movie *Lara Croft Tomb Raider* with Angelina Jolie. Supposedly she hung out there, but I looked everywhere, and much to my chagrin, I failed to spot her. What a letdown. After lunch, the girls opted for a massage while we boys walked around town to kill an hour.

As we slowly strolled and investigated, we spotted a number of concrete-encased tanks full of water. We saw people sitting on the edge of the concrete with their feet in the water. As we got closer we noticed that there were fish in the tanks, and the attendant explained that the fish were eating the dead skin off the people's feet, which, according to him, had some type of therapeutic value. Steve and I decided to pay the three dollars to stick our feet into a fish tank, even though we had lived this long with the presumed dead skin on our feet with no ill effects. We removed our shoes, sat on the edge, and put our feet into the water. Almost immediately hordes of fish descended upon us and began to nip at our feet. It was amazingly ticklish, almost unbearable for the first twenty or thirty seconds, then we became acclimated and it became merely annoying. The swarms of small (five to ten inches long) fish were relentless in their pursuit of our dead skin. The attendant saw that we were quickly getting bored with this, so he decided that our interest level might heighten if he supplied each of us with a free beer. He was right. We hung around longer than we would have without the beer, and other passersby saw us enjoying the beer and nibbles, so they too opted for a space on the edge. We had now become a marketing tool. Evidently this was a big thing in Siem Reap, as there were many places that did that. But if you think about it, the patrons were paying the owner three dollars each to feed

42. Hanging Out in Town

their fish. It seemed like an all-profit situation, and maybe it would be a good investment to open a "dead skin nipping spot" on Miami Beach; although, just maybe, the Health Department or code enforcement people might have a say in the matter. The girls met us after their massage for one more drink and one more shopping spree into and out of the many shops in town. They raved about their massages and said they felt much better now and the soreness from all the walks and climbing in the ruins was gone.

We then rode a tuk-tuk back to the hotel to get ready for our last group dinner with Mark, our cruise director, and the rest of the passengers. The bus loaded up exactly at 7:15, as everything came off precisely as planned and strictly on time on this tour. We headed over to La Tradition de Angkor restaurant, and got off the bus amidst flaming torches and spear-bearing local restaurant guards. We were seated at long tables placed in front of a gilded stage. From behind the side curtains appeared beautiful, heavily made-up young Cambodian dancers in full regalia. They did a traditional Khmer dance, after which the audience politely applauded, then the dancers came back out for a bow, but since they had already been applauded at the end of their dance, no one clapped again. They need to straighten that out.

The dances were what was referred to as an "Asparas Dance Show." The show included exhibitions of the four genres of traditional Khmer dancing: Asparas Dance, Masked Dance, Shadow Theater, and Folk Dance.

Fish nibbling the dead skin off my feet in Siem Reap. Not a bad deal for three dollars, and I got a cold beer too.

Native Cambodian dancers performing inside the La Tradicion de Angkor Restaurant in Siem Reap. The show was as good as the food ... fantastic.

There was a costume change between each. This was not just four simple disparate dances, but they were meant to convey a story or message. The dancers were subtle and somewhat restrained in their movements. The costuming was ornate, with multicolored silk robes and gowns and high golden-colored head pieces. The dancers' posture was taut, their backs and feet arched, fingers flexed, facial expressions matching each other almost exactly, and they moved sensuously with slow, deliberate, flowing movements. The dances were all inspired by the *Reamker*, a Cambodian epic poem that adapted Hindu ideas to Buddhist themes, showing the balance of good and evil in the world.

Food was then served, starting with green mango salad with smoked fish, and a spring roll. After that course, another dance routine ensued with more misplaced applause, and then another course of the meal was served consisting of Cambodian koh-koh soup with coconut cream, then more dancing and more inappropriately placed applause. Next, a course of barbecued beef on lemon grass skewers was served, and along with the beef were traditional fish, chicken, pork, vegetables, and rice.

The presentation as well as the food was outrageous at La Tradicion. This was just one of many servings of small appetizer-like plates that we were served.

Following that course, there was another dance routine, then we finished up the meal with a "symphony" of Cambodian sweets and fruit, and of course one more round of off-timed applause. All in all, it was quite an entertaining evening with an array of flavors that delighted the taste buds of everyone. From there we headed back to the hotel, where those leaving the next day said their goodbyes, even though we would all be having breakfast together in the morning.

43

THE INCIDENTS

    I was involved in three rather strange noncombat incidents (other than delivering a baby) while serving with the Navy in Vietnam. Two of them ended up costing the Navy money, in the form of restitution for damaged goods or lost property. The third involved only me and a couple of misguided Army MPs. I deny any personal guilt in all three.

    The incident involving only me started off simple enough. While stationed at the Cam Ranh Bay Naval Support Facility (NSF), it was not unusual for some sailors to adopt a pet, which in most cases would have been a dog. While it was rumored that the local Vietnamese often made meals of dogs, I never witnessed that, and tried to keep that particular vision out of my mental experience. My roommate, Jack, a tall, thin, very funny black guy from West Monroe, Louisiana, and I, had a small dog that we adopted. The dog was a gray and black mutt. He was small, somewhat cute, albeit a bit wolfish looking, caused us very little trouble, and was possibly the slowest-moving animal we had ever encountered. Because of this last trait, we naturally named him Lightning.

    The Navy's rule was, though, if we wanted to keep a dog, we would first have to drive across fifteen kilometers of sand dunes and hardpack roadway from the Navy base to visit the Army veterinarian at the huge Cam Ranh Bay Army Base. This was to make sure that the dog was not rabid, and had all of its up-to-date shots. I was elected to take Lightning over to the army base for his checkup.

    After an incident-free drive, and similar visit to the vet, I put Lightning into my jeep and headed back to NSF. On the way, before departing the army base, I opted to stop for a burger and a shake, to go, from the Army's on-base malt shop. The military was always trying to bring a little bit of "Americana" into the war. I ate the burger in the jeep as I drove, and on the way down the hardpack road to NSF, the paper wrapper evidently blew out of the jeep. Unconcerned at this minor triviality, I continued drinking my chocolate shake. Only seconds later, and seemingly out of nowhere, an Army MP jeep pulled up behind me, lights flashing, siren at full blast, and waved me over. Bear in mind, I was in a gray Navy jeep. Two strapping MPs, with white web belts, spit-polished shoes, and pants creased sharper than a Samurai sword, got out of the jeep. With billy clubs in their right hands, they slowly sauntered up beside me, crisply smacking the end of their clubs into the palms of their left hands. It was like a rerun of every redneck cop or prison movie I had ever seen.

"What's the problem?" I queried.

"Step out of the jeep, sailor," one of them replied tersely.

"What's the problem?" I again asked.

"We are going to have to write you a citation," smirked the shorter of the two.

"For what?" I said.

"Littering," said the taller one, with a straight, stoic face.

My eyebrows went up questioningly and I yelled, "Littering? In a war zone, with bomb craters, defoliated forests, crashed planes, rusting hulks of damaged jeeps, trucks, and tanks, and dead bodies all over the place ... littering? You're kidding, right?"

They weren't kidding. I was incredulous. They wrote me a citation and two weeks later I had to drive to the army base again and suffer the formality of an inquiry in front of the Army Provost Marshall. I had decided to represent myself, as there were no Navy attorneys available at my small base. Even if there had been, I doubt that any one of them would have jumped at the chance to defend me, as a littering case would, in most cases, not further their careers. After pleading my case, I was let off with a warning, because the Provost Marshall agreed with me that, being in the Navy, I was "probably" not familiar with Army regulations regarding littering in a war zone. After the hearing, he warned that "next time," they would not go so easily on me. This whole ordeal was most commonly known as the Army busting the Navy's balls. I tried to find other instances of "littering" charges against any American service men during the Vietnam War, but failed to find even one reference to it.

That was certainly a small, unimportant incident, but it has remained with me because of the complete absurdity of the situation. I mean, being charged with littering in a war zone ranks up there with, I don't know ... spitting in the ocean? Whenever I look back on my life and think of the most illogical and bizarre happenings that have occurred to me, that episode always places near the top of the list.

43. The Incidents

The second incident also took place in Cam Ranh Bay. It involved the fifty-foot LCM-6 boat that I piloted daily, to pick up and return the base workers to their village across the bay. The return trip from Bagnoi often took place after dark, depending on the time of the year. There was a curfew, after sundown, in Cam Ranh Bay, for any of the local fishing boats. They were strictly forbidden to be out on the water during non-daylight hours, as a precautionary step, so we knew that any and all boats on the bay after dark were military boats that could be kept track of. Anything else was considered to be the enemy.

After dropping off the workers, I turned the boat around and headed back to base, a forty-five-minute ride. I was driving the boat, and my crewman, Vinny, from Long Island, was standing high on the front ramp of the boat guiding me, using a flashlight for signaling purposes. That was done because when the boat was empty, the bow rode high in the water, and impeded the view directly in front of the boat from the pilothouse, which was situated in the stern. Fifteen minutes into the return trip I watched Vinny from my perch in the after part of the forty-ton boat as he began to frantically wave me to the right. He moved the flashlight frenetically, instructing me to give hard right rudder, which I did—but not before hearing a sickening crunch, and feeling a slight bump. I slowed the throttles of the two 6-72 Gray Marine diesel engines that powered the boat, and put the reduction gears into neutral, which then allowed me to hear what Vinny was yelling.

"You just ran over a small fishing boat, with two guys in it," he yelled back to me.

"What the hell were they doing there? It's after dark," I retorted.

"Fishing!" yelled Vinny, who then added, "but they jumped out before you hit them."

We plucked the scared and angry Vietnamese fishermen out of the water and made sure they were OK. I then radioed the Harbor Entrance Control Point (HECP), and our conversation went something like this:

"HECP, this is Lima Charlie Mike-five four, do you read?"

"Lima Charlie Mike-five four, this is HECP, we read, go ahead."

"HECP, Lima Charlie Mike-five four, made contact with South Vietnamese fishing boat, sunk same, over."

"Lima Charlie Mike-five four, HECP, you F'n what? Repeat your last!"

"HECP, this is Lima Charlie Mike-five four, made contact with South Vietnamese fishing boat, sunk same, over."

Well, they finally got the message and I was instructed to head for the harbormaster's dock to explain in full. I took the two fishermen, dropped them at the harbormaster's, and explained what happened. No fault was declared on my part, but the two fishermen collected eight hundred dollars from the Navy to pay for their small boat and received a stern warning never to go fishing at night again. Eight hundred dollars seemed fair for a hollowed-out tree trunk.

The third out-of-the-ordinary incident happened in the Mekong Delta while I was the captain of an LCM-8 boat. The boat was seventy feet long, weighed in at sixty-nine tons, and was powered by four 6-72 Gray Marine diesel engines. My three-man crew and I were two days out of Nha Be, our home base, on the Vam Co Tay River, heading for Moc Hoa (Mok-Wah). We were carrying supplies for the small advanced base, which included beer, soda, food, ammo, and various repair parts.

The rivers were never straight. There were always sharp turns and oxbows to deal with, so visibility was somewhat stunted along most of the cruise. As we rounded a turn in the river, the bow of my boat rose slightly out of the water, and the propellers made sounds that were not the usual sounds of propellers. They more closely resembled the sounds of a wood chipper, on low. Coinciding with this noise, we witnessed two Vietnamese farmers on the side of the river jumping up and down on the small dike that surrounded a nearby rice paddy. They were waving their hands and screaming wildly. I had no idea as to what was going on, and neither Dale, nor Dennis, nor Jack could figure it out.

I slowed the boat down and pulled over to the bank of the river. The Vietnamese gentlemen were screaming at me, and pointing into the water behind my boat. The water, which always had a brown hue, now had blood-red streaks running from my stern. I thought I had run over someone. I felt sickened, but none of us had seen anyone in the water. In a combat zone, we were used to keeping track of whatever was in our general area. We had learned that being aware of your immediate surroundings was a very good way to stay alive. Because of this motivation, we were unimaginably observant.

As we drifted slowly, a large carcass popped up behind the boat. We had run over the farmers' water buffalo. Water buffalos, in Vietnam, were equivalent in importance to an American farmer's John Deere tractor. They were an invaluable tool to the farmers for tilling the rice fields, and for producing milk, which is richer in fat and protein than that produced by dairy cattle. There are 130 million water buffalos, and it is a little-known fact that more human beings depend on them than any other domestic animal on earth. They range in height from four to five feet at the withers, and tip the scales anywhere from eight hundred to just over

43. The Incidents

two thousand pounds. They thrive mostly on aquatic plants, and more often than not, they graze submerged or semi-submerged in the rivers, with nothing visible but their black noses. This makes them very difficult to see in the dark-brown brackish water ... which is why we didn't.

The Navy ended up paying those two gentlemen twelve hundred dollars for the loss of their water buffalo, which is more money than either one of them could have made in a year, or maybe even two. I was not charged, but I was reprimanded. We were reminded, in no uncertain terms, that our job was to kill people, not buffalos. Evidently there was no monetary remuneration expected, or offered, for ending human life.

Those three incidents show just how singular war is. None of them could have happened to me under any other circumstances. I am happy to say that in the many years since those events took place, I have not once littered in a war zone, run over night fishermen with a boat, nor killed even one water buffalo.

44

BANGKOK AND THE END OF THE TRIPS

No early rising today in the hotel, as there were no outings planned and most of us were going our own separate ways; some to Bangkok, some to Hanoi, some to Bali. Our guide, Mark, was heading back to Saigon for yet another trip up the Mekong. After breakfast and a few last goodbyes, Steve, Debbie, Mary, and I packed and headed for the airport in Siem Reap for our flight to Bangkok. After interminable waits at the check in/out line, we boarded, and in fifty short minutes arrived at the busiest, most modern-looking airport I had ever encountered.

It was a breeze through passport check and customs, though, and we quickly boarded the Avalon bus for the forty-minute ride to the outrageously beautiful and modern Bangkok Intercontinental Hotel. It was a magnificent five-star edifice right downtown, ultra-modern with a beautifully designed lobby area.

Bangkok was a striking city, but in many ways it looked just like every other large city, with the exception of the raised pedestrian walkways that covered the downtown area. It was huge and bustling, with massive areas of traffic congestion and gigantic office, hotel, and condo towers everywhere. It was clean, though, and everything appeared to be brand-new. The streets were free of litter, the taxis were spotless, and everyone was well-dressed. Bangkok is the capital of Thailand and is located in the Chao Phraya River delta in central Thailand. The city occupies a little over six hundred square miles and has a population of just above eight million. It began as a small riverfront trading post during the fifteenth century Ayutthaya Kingdom and has grown to become the absolute center of politics, education, economy, and media in modern-day Thailand.

A complimentary drink was served in the bar while our room keys

44. Bangkok and the End of the Trips

Inside the new and ultramodern Bangkok International Airport, in Bangkok, Thailand, our place of departure.

were obtained by our new guide, Peter, and then up to our splendidly appointed five-star rooms, which required an electrical engineer in order to figure out how the lights worked. A one-room hotel suite really does not require upwards of twenty-five light and wall switches. It took a while, but we figured it out.

After a couple of hours of rest we met Steve and Debbie in the lobby and walked on the raised pedestrian walkway to dinner at a restaurant that was recommended by Peter. We actually found it, and ordered a table full of Thai specialties, including two different soups, deep-fried pork ribs, shrimp, chicken curry, shrimp fried rice, sautéed black mushrooms, and seven beers. This huge meal came out to seventy dollars for all four of us, quite a deal. Back to the hotel, a goodbye to Steve and Debs and up to bed for some rest to help deal with the ultra-long day coming up tomorrow.

As with all things good and bad, an end must come. When my one-year tour was almost up during my original trip to Southeast Asia, I was summoned into the base commander's office and offered a deal. At that point in my Navy career, I still had 18 months to go on my original four-year active enlistment. He told me how valuable I was to the war effort and that the Navy was willing to let me out of my final year of service if I voluntarily agreed to stay in Vietnam for another six months. In addition,

The lobby area in the Bangkok Intercontinental Hotel, a 5-star hotel in every way.

44. Bangkok and the End of the Trips

The elevated pedestrian walkway that traverses most of the downtown area of Bangkok, which keeps people safe, and off the automobile-infested highways and streets below.

they were offering me a $5,000 tax-free cash bonus if I agreed to stay. I thought about it for about seven milliseconds. Five grand was a lot of bucks to someone who was making $444 a month, which included an extra $65 "hostile fire pay," and another $65 for hazardous duty pay, because of my diving designation. I told the commander that I would agree under one condition. I told him I wanted off the rivers. I'm no fool. I said

Me in a sampan, up river on the Vam Co Dong, with our covered .50 caliber machine gun in the foreground.

that I would extend here if they sent me back to Cam Ranh Bay and let me resume my job as base diver. That was the job I was trained to do, and according to the Navy, it cost them $100,000 to send me through the twelve-week-long school to become certified and qualified as a Navy Diver. After all, I had managed to make it through nine months on the rivers,

Opposite, top: **Another picture of me in a sampan, almost getting the hang of it, looking steady … but don't let that fool you.** *Opposite, bottom:* **Sharing a sampan with a young local Vietnamese boy, who taught me how to maneuver the small dugout boat.**

44. Bangkok and the End of the Trips

having encountered numerous firefights, a couple of small injuries, one concussion, an exploded and sunken river boat, presentation of an award for being wounded in action, and nine months of really crappy food and sleeping conditions; not to mention the joy of living outdoors most of the time in a semi-tropical jungle.

Much to my surprise, and stifled glee, he agreed to that, and I was off to my barracks, packing my sea bag and weapons once again. I was bussed to Tan San Nhut Airport in Saigon the next day and flown back to Cam Ranh Bay. Most of the personnel who spent their entire tours in Cam Ranh had never gotten involved in actual combat. NSF was a repair facility, and most of the men stationed there were, for lack of a better description, tradespeople. They had specialized skills that were utilized in the maintenance and repair of small boats and engines. They were welders, painters, mechanics, metal workers, woodworkers, and electronics technicians. They grilled me constantly about what it was like on the rivers, what it was like to get shot at, and to shoot at others. They asked me if I was afraid while there. I told them that I was constantly afraid and scared for my life and the lives of my crew.

For the next six months I was the senior diver (out of two of us) and made over 150 dives of all types. I repaired small boats, found lost items, set up an underwater lighting system around the dock area, retrieved bodies, and blew up boats that had been sunk and were impeding river traffic all up and down the central coast. Being back in Cam Ranh was like being on vacation compared to riding the rivers. It was akin to moving into the Ritz Carlton after spending time at Motel 6. Although I must admit, except for the crappy food, being shot at, and having to kill other human beings, the river experience was similar to the nine-to-five job in Cam Ranh. But even on the rivers we sometimes had time to enjoy some recreational experiences, like having a local boy teach us how to use a sampan. Sometimes it worked out, and sometimes it didn't. Cam Ranh even had a softball field where we played ball a few days a week. It was nice to have some of the basic amenities of life again, such as a roof, a door, air conditioning, warm food, toilets, sinks, and of course weekends off.

Leaving the war in Vietnam, and back in the world today, Mary and I awakened at 4:30 a.m. in Bangkok, so that we could meet Peter in the lobby at 5:30. He was right on time, obtained us each a boxed breakfast, and then we were off to the airport. A half hour later, Peter took our luggage into the terminal, showed us the proper line to check in, and that marked the official end of the Avalon Tours part of our trip. There was still the twenty-five-hour flight home. Most of it was as pleasant as sitting

44. Bangkok and the End of the Trips

Me getting ready to put one over the fence at the softball field at the Cam Ranh Bay Naval Support Facility.

in the same position for hours on end can be. Cathay Pacific Airlines tried to make one's voyage with them as comfortable and as enjoyable as possible.

Unfortunately, the same could not be said for American Airlines, whose motto should be, "American Airlines—We'll Get You There, but It Won't Be Pleasant!" I'm not sure if it is because American has the oldest employees in the business, and they were just tired of doing what they were doing, or because American required a total lack of charm and people skills in the personnel they chose to represent them, but they are just not a friendly company. After the efficiently served and somewhat tasty meals on all Cathay Pacific and Thai Airways flights, our five-hour flight from Los Angeles to Miami was a letdown. They served one drink and one bag of peanuts as their meal, and sold sandwiches to anyone who wanted one.

But enough about flying. We made it back to Miami, picked up our luggage, and arrived at our home to officially end the trip.

45

ENTERTAINMENT

According to the U.S. government's "Combat Area Casualty File" (CACF), the belief that the fighting in Vietnam was not as intense as the fighting during World War II is a total inaccuracy. The facts are that infantrymen in the South Pacific during World War II engaged in an average of forty days of combat in four years, while the average infantryman in Vietnam saw an average of two hundred and forty days of combat in one year, while the average river patrol boat crew saw an average of one hundred seventy-five days of combat during the same year. That was a startling difference, and one that the majority of the American public is almost completely unaware of.

The U.S. military, in all of its inherent wisdom, realized that being involved in some type of combat situation on an almost daily basis for a year created high stress levels in the participants. I have no doubt that they did a multimillion-dollar study to come up with that more-than-obvious hypothesis. One can only imagine the meeting that took place, and the conversation that led to this revelation.

"So, Bob, what do you think the effects on an individual would be if you placed him in a situation where he was fully aware that groups of hidden enemy combatants were attempting to kill or harm him on a daily basis?"

"Hmm, not positive about this, Jim, but I think that besides making him a bit nervous, he might encounter the effects of stress over that period of time."

"Sounds good to me, Bob, write a report and submit it."

Although I am paraphrasing, taking it down to its basest level, it had to go something like that. The military has always been rife with the obvious, even though they might have looked at it as reasonable or even groundbreaking.

45. Entertainment

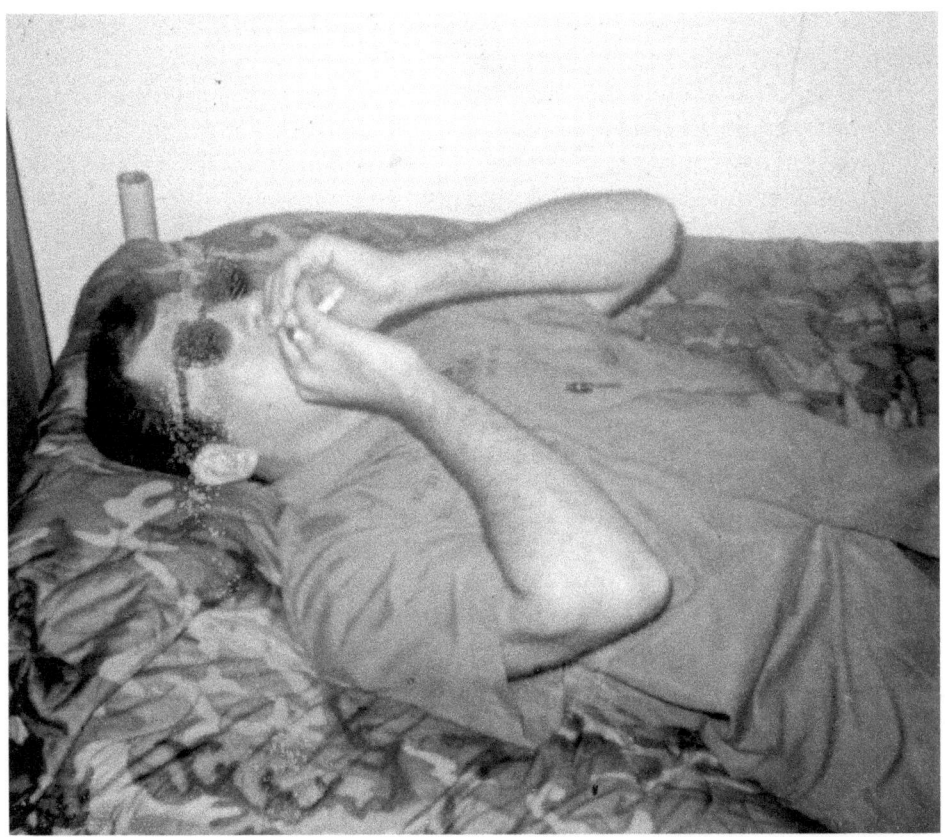

Me taking a break by partaking in the "in-country" national pastime. Sometimes one just had to mellow out in order to deal with the everyday happenings in a war zone.

As stated earlier, one of the purported solutions to the stress problem was granting a week or so of Rest & Relaxation (R & R) to all those who had served at least six months in Vietnam. Those few days were supposed to ease or completely erase the effects of the approximately hundred and twenty days of combat during the first six months, and give a fresh new start, both physically and mentally, to the upcoming final hundred and twenty days of combat in the next six months.

The ludicrousness of this way of thinking is well documented and evidenced by the thousands of cases of post-traumatic stress disorder (PTSD) suffered by many of the men after their release from the military or their movement to another duty station outside the war zone. PTSD was not invented by or unique to Vietnam veterans. In wars past it was called hysteria, soldier's heart, irritable heart, DaCosta's syndrome, railway spine, fright neuroses, combat stress reaction, stress response syndrome, shell shock, and numerous other names. An automobile accident, rape, or other traumatic event also can cause it. It is not limited to males. It does not have to be war-related. The Vietnam War helped medical progress in this area.

Going back, we see that in 1904, Frenchman Pierre Janet proposed that "when people experience 'vehement emotions,' the mind might not be able to match what is going on with existing cognitive schemes. As a result, memories of the experience cannot be integrated into personal awareness. Instead, they are split off (dissociated) from conscious awareness and from voluntary control." Thus the first comprehensive formulation of the effects of trauma on the mind was recorded. This was based on the notion that failure to integrate traumatic memories due to extreme emotional arousal results in the symptoms of what we today call PTSD.

The military dealt with the debilitating effects of PTSD, as well as other stress-related conditions during the war, in many ways. In addition to the military's steps toward the reduction of the effects of stress, many individuals took it upon themselves to deal with it in their own special ways. Some of those methods were frowned upon by the military, but many were overlooked or completely ignored. It was my observation that alcoholism was an accepted side effect of being in the military, as few were treated and even fewer were prosecuted for acts induced by the overuse of alcohol. With beer costing a dime and mixed drinks a few cents more, it was a simple act to get buzzed on a dollar at any of the enlisted or officer's clubs. As we see below, I personally chose another way of dealing with the everyday stress caused by the fear of imminent loss of an important body part, or of my life.

Other men used various additional methods of dealing with their stress levels. Some used heroin, some used opium, and many others used alcohol, due to its abundant and easy accessibility, as well as its legality and cheap military price. I never used any of those, as the idea of sticking a needle in my own arm was completely abhorrent to me, and visiting an opium den was out of the question after the horror stories I heard about the quality of the people I might come across inside one. Fortunately for me, I never acquired a taste for alcohol, other than the occasional cold beer on a hot day. Therefore, since I was from Miami, it only seemed natural that marijuana would become my personal "stress reliever" of choice. To paraphrase American Express, "We never left on patrol without it." It was cheap and readily available, although rolling papers were scarce. To

45. Entertainment

Aboard a U.S. naval ship off the coast of Cam Ranh Bay, in the South China Sea, we watched Raquel Welch and other performers perform for the troops. We rode out there in our own boats.

counter this, most of us owned one of the aforementioned corncob pipes that we carried everywhere.

There were other ways that the military dealt with the inherent stress. One of those was the traveling USO show. Many celebrities and entertainment stars gave of their time to tour the war zone with their minions of staff and bands. This was mostly a magnanimous offer on their parts as, besides travel costs, they donated their time and talent in order to offer the troops a respite from their everyday chores and battles. These shows were greatly and appreciatively received by the troops who attended and did offer a sort of short-time "normalness" to the troops' existence, as well as a tie to "the real world." On one occasion I even took my boat, filled with other men from the base, from Cam Ranh Bay out into the ocean to watch a show aboard an aircraft carrier. We got to see Raquel Welch, in her prime, put on a greatly appreciated and well-received show. Who knew she could sing? Who cared that she could sing?

Along with the government-sponsored USO shows, there were other forms of entertainment offered the troops, covering a wide range of entertainment genres. Some were rock

One of the many dancing and performing groups that toured the military bases and were there to raise the morale of the troops. It worked!

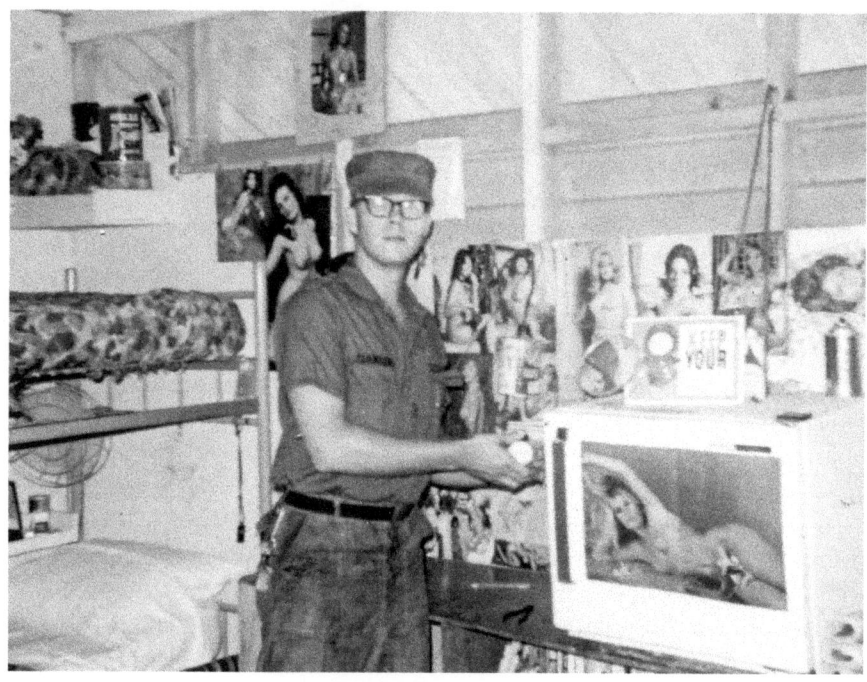

Opposite, bottom and above: **Wall decorations in barracks rooms. Preferences varied, but the overall theme seemed to be the same wherever one went.**

bands, country bands, or what is commonly referred to as "dancing girls." The bands were great, as Asian bands, and more specifically Filipino, Japanese and Vietnamese bands were masters of copying. They could perform songs and music that exactly replicated the voices and sounds of the original singers, whether they were the Doors, the Beatles, the Stones, Janis Joplin, Grace Slick, or any number of American country and western performers. They were incredible. Their presentation was a bit different, but the music was right-on. The lead singers were usually fancy-dressed females, with traditionally dressed backup bands.

Left: Me showing off some of the more personal items sent to us from "acquaintances" back home. Some were kept private. *Right:* My roommate showing off some of those more personal gifts received from girlfriends, wives, or acquaintances back in "the world." Some were put in more public places for others to enjoy.

The "dancing girl" acts were a bit different, offering some visual relief for the troops, who, depending on where they were stationed, were usually sexually starved individuals.

Taking the whole entertainment thing a bit further, some of the troops instituted the option of decorating their "hootches" (barracks living compartments) in their own particular mode. A majority of the decorating involved innovative wallpapering of the interior walls of the two-man barracks rooms, and seemed to be motivated by a central theme.

As has been plainly shown, the U.S. government, and particularly the military arm of the government, was always on the cutting edge of finding and supplying an abundant array of differing varieties of entertainment for its hard-fighting troops. Those reprieves from the dangers and frustrations of the everyday life encounters of the combat troops offered a chance to smile, a chance to sing along, a chance to witness some of the things that take place in a normal world, a world devoid of constant death, destruction, horror, and carnage, which, without the diversions, would certainly become the norm.

45. Entertainment

Other forms of entertainment circulated throughout the war zone at any given time. Comedians, revues, magicians, solo artists, and even military bands traveled around playing for those who needed any type of departure from the daily grind and boredom caused by being stationed in and rooted to a particular area and job. All of those who gave of their time to amuse, arouse, and entertain the troops were greatly appreciated, not only for their inherent talents, but also for the mere fact that they were there.

The last area of entertainment, or search for normalcy in that highly abnormal life situation, was a bit more personal. Those men who had wives or girlfriends, or sometimes just pen pals, back in "the world," received not only cookies, cakes, and other homemade and packaged "goody boxes" from home, but often received objects of a much more personal nature. These were often times put on display for others to ogle and appreciate, and always brought a smile to those entering the rooms that displayed them.

As you can see, entertainment, in its many facets, played a huge part in attempting to heighten the morale of the troops. It did make for a little bond with the real world and kept us all thinking that the entire world was not crazy, that war was not the normal state of things, and that better things will come.

46

WAR?

What I speak about in this chapter, in reference to my actions, and the actions of others that I witnessed during the Vietnam War, reflects merely my own observations and musings garnered from my personal encounters as a participant. During the war I was lucky enough to have kept a notebook of my experiences and the experiences of some of those that I encountered. I was also fortunate in that all of my friends and family members saved the letters I had written them from the various places I had the opportunity to visit. They returned them to me upon my homecoming, and those letters have been an invaluable source of reminding me of some of the events and actions that I certainly would not have remembered had they not been available. The letters are now safely stored in a notebook on my bookshelf.

More than any other form of human contact, war has a lifelong effect on the people who were encompassed by it and were fortunate, or in some cases unfortunate, enough to have lived through it. The consequences of war on every individual involved are long-lasting, no matter what aspect of the conflict they were involved in. Of course, the soldiers themselves, having been thrust into a situation that was totally alien to any other undertaking that they have had, or will confront, in their normal lives, were among the hardest hit both physically and psychologically. I think that the majority of the men that I ran into, who acclimated themselves to the situation best, were the guys who had prior inner-city gang connections and the guys who lived in rural areas that were comfortable with hunting and shooting. Ground and river combat basically boiled down to "hunting and shooting."

Throughout the ages, the majority of men who found themselves involved in actual combat, whether it be with rocks, spears, bows and arrows, conventional firearms, or ultramodern chemical and nuclear weapons, have historically been young men. Their leaders and the men who instigated the wars were older, but the actual fighting man was, and is, typically in his late teens to late twenties. The average age of the Vietnam combat soldier was 21.8 years old, and the average age of the fifty-eight thousand one hundred forty-eight men who were killed in Vietnam was 22.1 years. This was surely due to the fact that anyone older than that invariably had enough sense, or status and social power, not to involve himself on a personal level in such a disastrous and damaging venture. But since the mindset of the young aggressive male dictated "I am invincible," then he was the perfect pawn for the old men who started and administered wars.

Being young and invincible gave rise to the consideration that while holding a weapon, you were not only indestructible; you were also the supreme ruler of any immediate space that you happened to be occupying. It was this very attitude that customarily caused the most calamitous problems for the indigenous population of any area occupied by those young, unshakable mini-rulers.

In any war-torn country or region, there are going to be varying population centers, ranging from metropolitan areas or large cities, to small rural outposts or villages, all the way down to very sparsely populated settlements and hamlets. Where one lived during a time of conflict had an effect of great magnitude in determining just what the results of war would be on that individual. It appeared to me that in larger, more populated centers, the individual soldier still seemed to be guided, generally, by the rules, regulations, and mores that he grew up with in his family environment, and those behaviors generally accepted in a normal society. Throughout the world, with a few exceptions, there are certain rules of society that appear to be universal. Most large metropolitan areas of the world frown on such things as murder, rape, robbery, arson and other such criminal activity.

To the contrary, in smaller, rural areas, the individual soldier would, more likely, take on this "mini-ruler" mindset. In those outlying areas, there no longer were policies and regulations that must be followed as if in a civilized society. This "little village" wasn't really civilized society; it was far removed and the same rules didn't necessarily have to be applied there. No one was watching and there was little chance of consequences for acting out of societal norms. The pent-up anger and rage that were inherent in most fighting men, due usually to the loss of buddies or friends who had been killed or injured, reared its ugly head, and woe be to the person or persons who got in the way. In many cases it was almost impossible to differentiate between friend and foe in the jungles of Vietnam; a farmer by day was a Viet Cong by night. Who was the enemy, and who was not? This was a situation that constantly arose, and many soldiers decided to act on the safer side of valor. What was one more "inconsequential" death among the thousands? This attitude made it even easier to act out. When you eliminated the repercussions for deviant or depraved and immoral behavior, those activities flourished, and some decisions became easier to make. My boat crews and I knew that we were free to do as we saw fit in any up-river situation. We knew that had we decided to indiscriminately shoot everyone we saw along the river, or stop and loot the small villages, or take advantage of the many women we came across, nothing would become of it. We would not have been held accountable for our actions, for no one would ever know ... but us. We collectively decided that that was enough incentive. We didn't want to carry such a burden with us, long after we left here. We "behaved."

Situations such as those just described gave way to the many accounts of brutality and various other forms of one man's inhumanity toward another. Most of those instances have never come to light. It was chilling what some persons were capable of doing to others, solely because they had the power to do so. Jewelry, money, personal belongings, women, life itself ... all of those things became nothing more than the spoils of war to the invading victor, to take or use as he wished. That was especially the case if he was but a temporary victor or a passerby, for he would soon be gone. It was very easy to see how multitudes of persons could be affected by the actions of one, or a few.

Only a small number of happy stories come out of war. But few writers who covered conflicts were looking for happy stories. If they were, they wouldn't have been in a war zone, using combat as a backdrop for their writings. The thing about war writing is that it continually became easier and easier as the war progressed, due to the fact that everyone had a story to tell: the soldier, the leader, the victims, the raped, the plundered, the pillaged. They all had a story, and their numbers increased exponentially as the war progressed. Every country, every city, every village, every street, and every home that has seen war has a story.

Many of the men who served in my war had major psychological problems after returning home. You've all heard of the "crazed Vietnam veteran," made so popular in a multitude of movies and books. Thank you, Rambo! My theory on that is that not only did they suffer from the trauma of combat (PTSD) in general, but additional factors came into play. They did things there that, at the time, seemed to be OK or acceptable because of their skewed sense of what actually was acceptable. But, later, after returning to their homes, their jobs, and their families, they began to reflect upon some of those episodes they were involved in or witnessed. They recalled those occasions where they had choices, and the actions they participated in that were over and above their normal combat duties. They took advantage of others who could not defend themselves. They killed for sport. Those were the things that nightmares were made of. Those were the things that would keep a man in therapy for life. Guilt is a terrible thing to live with ... forever.

Having been personally affected by being involved in a war, and in combat, I am constantly looking back. I am satisfied with my own actions and decisions, and how I reacted to some of the opportunities presented to me: those acts that would have had no repercussions, at the time, had I gone along with the basest of human instincts. I can say, though, without reservation, that I did nothing that I could not tell my mother about. I never murdered anyone. I never raped anyone, and I never stole anything from anyone. Although opportunities arose on numerous occasions to partake in any of those endeavors, there were a great many men, like my crewmates and me, who did not succumb to the temptations, and returned home to lead happy and productive lives, affected only by what we saw, not by what we did. We looked at it as a temporary job, an inconvenient, although interesting and exciting, pothole in the journey of life, and looked forward to going home and getting on with our "real" lives.

I feel strengthened by my war experiences. I have come to realize, after being in a prolonged situation where my life was in danger day after day, common everyday problems that have arisen since the war just haven't measured up in intensity level. Or, as my mother so succinctly put it, "Just get over it and move on." I learned to deal with adversity and horror, and situations that required instantaneous decision making. I learned to trust myself and my ability to analyze a situation, and then seek and find solutions quickly. This learned attribute was an invaluable tool in the thirty-seven years that I owned and operated a business. I also learned to live, if but only momentarily, in the shoes of those I encountered, and allowed them to enter my decision-making processes. Failure to take into account what effect your actions might have on others is a flawed decision-making strategy; flawed, in that it becomes haunting and eternal. If during a time of monumental and widespread hostilities and barbarity one can fight for his life on a daily basis, against an enemy doing the same, and maintain a modicum of decency toward his fellow man, he has passed the most important tests of war.

What can I say about returning to the place that solidified my nearly lifelong standing as a born-again agnostic, or more exactly, a secular humanist. There couldn't possibly be a God after what I saw going on in Vietnam in the late 1960s. God would never have allowed that, for he/she has always been described as a "just and good God." There was nothing just and there was nothing good going on in Vietnam. My return helped alter the thoughts and visions that came to mind every time I remembered or reflected on Vietnam. Now, I see it as a happy, vibrant place, a feeling which could not help but spill over into the consciousness of anyone who visited.

As we traveled the rivers on the luxurious Angkor cruise boat, I found myself interacting with the young man I once was, so many years ago … right there, right in that exact spot. I was seeing the same places through different eyes, places once rife with turmoil and chaos. I smelled the same scents, the nuc mam and the humid jungle. I was seeing the people who had not outwardly changed, with their black pajamas, sandals, and conical hats. I talked with that young man and told him that it had all worked out well. I was happy and satisfied with what he did, how he acted, and with his frame of mind when he left there. I had come home, and the few nightmares and recurring visions had dissipated over time. I let him know that I had meshed back into society in spite of what I thought, at one point, would be intrusive images never to be erased. Those visions now are of beautiful, wide boulevards, people harvesting the country's riches, and the same jungle … but now, peaceful, serene, and safe. We, unlike ill-fated thousands, had made it.

Acronyms and Foreign Words

ACTOV   Accelerated Turn Over to the Vietnamese
AGER   Experimental Research Ship
AK (as in AK-47)   Avtomat Kalashnikov (Kalashnikov's automatic rifle, Russian)
AO   Area of Operation
Ao-Dai   ankle-to-waist slit tunic worn by Vietnamese women, over pants
ASPB   Assault Support Patrol Boat
ATC   Armored Troop Carrier
ATSB   Advanced Tactical Support Base
AWOL   Absent Without Leave
BUPERS   Bureau of Personnel
CACF   Combat Area Casualty File
Click   Kilometer
CPK   Communist Party of Kampuchia
C-RATS   Canned Rations
CT   Communication Technician
DOT   Department of Transportation
HUEY   UH-1B Helicopter
IUWG   Inshore Undersea Warfare Group
LARC   Lighter, Amphibious Resupply Cargo
LCM   Landing Craft Mechanized
M   Mark; designates version of a model, M-16, M-79, M-14, etc.
MAC   Military Air command
MACV-SOG   Military Assistance Command Vietnam Studies and Observation Group
MIA   Missing in Action
MOS   Military Occupational Specialty
MPC   Military Payment Certificate
MRF   Mobile Riverine Force

NSF   Naval Support Facility
NSU   Nonspecific Urethritis
Nuc-mam   Fish sauce extracted from fermented fish and salt
OSHA   Occupational Safety and Health Administration
PACV   Patrol Air-Cushion Vehicle
PBR   Patrol Boat River
PO   Petty Officer
POW   Prisoner Of War
PSY-OPS   Psychological Operations
PTSD   Post Traumatic Stress Disorder
PX   Post Exchange
R&R   Rest and Relaxation
RAF   Royal Air Force
SERE   Survival, Escape, Resistance, and Evasion
SRF   Ship Repair Facility
TRE   Target Rich Environment
USN   United States Navy
VC   Viet Cong
VHPA   Vietnam Helicopter Pilots Association

INDEX

Page numbers in ***bold italics*** indicate pages with illustrations.

Accelerated Turn Over to the Vietnamese (ACTOV) 215
Advanced Tactical Support Base 6, 93, 97
Agent Orange 99
AK-47 6, 75, 109, ***140, 141***
Alpha Boat 6, 60
American Airlines 12, 14, 15, 235
Angkor Ban ***153, 155, 156***
Angkor Thom ***194***
Angkor Wat 211–214, ***212–214***
Apocalypse Now 9
Avalon 44, 66
Avalon Angkor ***86, 106***, 111, ***112***, 120, 125, 150, ***164***

B-40 Rocket 6, 75, 109
Bangkok 228, ***229, 230, 231***
USS *Banner* **21**, 22, 28, 33
Bar Girls 25
Battle of Tsushima 48
Ben Thanh Market 54, ***56***
Boat Sinking 157
Booby Traps 73, ***74***, 75
Boot Camp 20
Buddhist Temple 125, ***126, 127, 153, 154***, 163, ***166, 167, 180***
Bullet Hole ***7***

C-4 Explosives 31
C-Rations 67, 68
Cai Be 112, ***113, 114, 115, 116, 117***
Cam Ranh Bay 13, 37, 43, 45, ***47***, 48, 65, 67, 146, 184, 203–210, 223, ***235***
Cambodia 5, 79, 125, 127, 150, ***191, 192***
Cambodian Dancers ***142, 143, 144***
Cathay Pacific 14, 15, 17
China 23
Cleveland National Forest 38
Communication Technicians 22
Congee 17

Coronado 35
Cu Chi (tunnels) 69, 70, ***73, 74, 76***
Culinary Arts Center 55, ***57***

Death Counts 15
Dive School 28, 29, ***33***
Diving 28, 29, ***32, 35, 206, 207***
Draft 19, 20

Eiffel, Gustav 86
Electrical Wires ***58***
Eskimo 108

Fairbanks, AK 21
Fifty Calibre Machine Gun 4, ***5***, 62
Fifty-One Calibre Machine Gun 6
Floating Homes ***121***
Fried Tarantulas ***193***

Geneva Convention ***36***, 39
Golden Triangle 106

Harbor Entrance Contorl Point (HECP) 225
Ho Chi Minh City 14, 17
Ho Chi Minh Train 79
Hoi An Restaurant 66, ***67***
Honeywell Grenade Launcher 63
Huey 4

Indochine Restaurant 75, ***76, 77***
Induction Center 19
Inshore Undersea Warfare Group 35, 36

Japan 21, 24
John 3

Kampong Tralech 179, ***181, 182***
Khmer Rouge 133, 135, 137–138
Killing Fields ***133, 134, 136, 137***
Kipling 11

251

252 Index

LCM-6 Boat 5, 65, **98**, **100**, **102**, **118**, 146
LCM-8 Boat 62, **63**, 226
Lighter, Amphibious Resupply Cargo (LARC) 147, 149
Littering 224
USS *Long Beach* 34
LSD 13

M-16 Machine Gun 4, 10, 62, 75, **91**, 110
M-60 Machine Gun 4, 62, 75, 130
M-79 Grenade Launcher 4, 63, 75, 90, **91**
Mangroves **159**, **160**
Marijuana 3, **64**, 185, **237**
Mekong Delta 6, 10, 11, 17, 71, 106, 226
Mekong River 104, 105, 196
Miami 10, 22, 48, 125, 161
Miami International Airport 12
Military Code of Conduct 39
Military haircut 20
Military Payment Certificate (MPC) **187**
Mini-Gun 4, 130
Mr. Nam 69, **71**, 72
Mobile Riverine Force 5, 62, 79
Moc Hoa 5
Monitor Boat 6, 60, **61**

Nantasket 24
Napalm 171
Native Fishing Boat **173**, **174**
Naval Enlistment **46**
Nguyen Van Thieu 51
Nha Be 60, 62, 67, 88, **89**, **90**, 93, 94, 96, 107, 131, 162, 215
Nixon, Richard 6
North Korea 23
North Vietnamese Tank **51**

Olongapo 30, 34
Operation Giant Slingshot 79, **80**
Operation Ranch Hand 98
Ox-Cart **181**

Parrot's Beak 79
Patrol Air-Cushion Vehicle (PACV) **197**
Phnom Penh **132**
Post Traumatic Stress Disorder (PTSD) 237, 238
POW Camp 39, 40
Presidential Palace **50**
Psychiatrist 36
USS *Pueblo* 23

R&R 175–178
Recon Marines 34

Remedios **30**, **31**
Rex Hotel 49
Rubber Trees **70**
Rung Sat Special Zone 98
Russians 22

Saigon 9, 17, 49, 60
Saigon Post Office 85
Saigon River 64, 65, **88**
San Diego 20, 38, 41
San Francisco 14
Sasebo 23
SEAL Team 97, 98, 100, **101**, 102
2nd Class Petty Officer **82**, **83**
SERE Training 37, 38, 39, **41**, **42**
Sex Cards **26**
Siem Reap 190, 201, 218–222
Silk Weaving **151**, **152**
Sniper 139
Stein, Steve, and Debbie 44, 49, 66, 75, 127
Stilt Homes **122**, **123**
Subic Bay 25, 28

Tan San Nhut 18
Tango Boat 6, 60, **62**, **198**
Target Rich Environment 170
Tiger Cage **54**
Tokyo Rose 23
Tonkin Gulf 46
Touiche Restaurant 201
Treasure Island 21
Tuyen Nhon 128, **130**

Vam Co Dong River 72, 79, **232**, **233**
Vam Co Tay River 5, 79, 128, 215, 226
Victoria Angkor Hotel **202**
Viet Cong 69, 70, 71, 72, 73, 97, 128
Vladivostok 22

War 10, 13
War Museum, Saigon **52**, 53, **55**
Warner Springs 38
Wat Han Che 163
Water Buffalo 226, 227
Welch, Raquel **239**
World Airways 15, 45

Yeoman 20, 28
Yokosuka 21, 22, 23

Zippo Boat 170

www.ingramcontent.com/pod-product-compliance
Ingram Content Group UK Ltd.
Pitfield, Milton Keynes, MK11 3LW, UK
UKHW041936140426
5217IPUK00014B/503